Sam Allberry has written a wonderful book on the significance of the resurrection. Full of great images, clearly organized, encouraging, humorous, biblical, insightful – I could go on. Reading this little volume on a central but neglected topic will benefit your life. If you would like more assurance, transformation, hope and purpose, this book shows you how we get all that from the resurrection of Christ.

—**Mark Dever**, *Pastor, Capitol Hill Baptist Church,*
    Washington DC

I think this book rocks! All Christian people need to know the great joy of living in the light of the resurrection of Jesus Christ from the dead. Sam Allberry has done us all a favour in writing such an engaging and readable book about such a vital subject. It is by turns amusing, moving, encouraging and profound. Writing out of his years of ministry to university students and from his own Christian experience, Sam helps us to look to a familiar horizon with fresh eyes. *Lifted* is a book that could easily form the centre of a discussion group, but individual readers will be – well, 'lifted'! – by what they find here.

—**Dr Michael Jensen**, *Lecturer in Christian Doctrine, Moore*
    College, Sydney and author of You: An Introduction

Lots of Christians discuss and think about the effect of Jesus' death on their lives, but many seem to be confused about how the resurrection fits into the picture. *Lifted* will help Christians of all ages and stages worship the Jesus who really is alive for the glorious hope he offers us.

—**Maurice and Anna McCracken,** *UCCF Relay Co-ordinators*

Very fresh and accessible – full of nice personal illustration and clear explanation.

—**Mark Meynell,** *Senior Associate Minister, All Souls Church,*
    Langham Place, London

Exactly what we need: joy-giving gospel truth, served up garden fresh. Read and rejoice!

—**Michael Reeves,** *Theological Advisor for UCCF*

Sixty years ago, the night I came to know that Jesus, God's beloved Son, had so loved *me* that he died for *my* sins, I was given Philippians 3:10 as my new life's verse: 'That I may know [Christ], and *the power of his resurrection*, and the fellowship of his sufferings . . . ' (AV, my emphasis). After reading this book, *Lifted*, by Sam Allberry, I feel I have at last entered into a full (or at least, a fuller) understanding of knowing 'the power of his resurrection'. I am only sorry I did not read this book many years ago!

—**Dr Helen Roseveare,** *author and former missionary*

It is extraordinary that there are relatively few books that focus on the vital implications of Jesus' resurrection. This book helps to plug that gap with a much-needed introduction to what the resurrection has accomplished for us. Sam Allberry peppers good teaching with engaging illustrations which make this a very helpful book for everyone who wants to re-examine this truth.

—**Adrian Warnock,** *blogger and author of* Raised with Christ: How the Resurrection Changes Everything

Lifted

Experiencing the
Resurrection Life

SAM ALLBERRY

R&R
PUBLISHING
P.O. BOX 817 • PHILLIPSBURG • NEW JERSEY 08865-0817

First published in the UK by Inter-Varsity Press 2010

North American edition issued 2012 by P&R Publishing

Printed in the United States of America

Library of Congress Cataloging-in-Publication Data
Allberry, Sam.
  Lifted : experiencing the resurrection life / Sam Allberry. -- North American ed.
    p. cm.
  Originally published: Nottingham, England : Inter-Varsity Press, 2010.
  Includes bibliographical references (p.   ).
  ISBN 978-1-59638-431-6 (pbk.)
  1. Jesus Christ--Resurrection. 2. Christian life. I. Title.
  BT482.A45 2012
  232'.5--dc23
                            2012000859

Contents

To my parents,
with much love
and gratitude

Foreword

IT USED TO BE SAID that teaching about the Holy Spirit was the Cinderella of Christian doctrines. If that was ever true, it certainly isn't now. But the resurrection of Christ would have a much better claim to that title. There are plenty of books and sermons that outline the arguments for its historicity but very few that explain its significance, despite the fact that the New Testament writers proclaim again and again that everything has changed now that Christ is risen. I warmly welcome this excellent book by Sam Allberry and pray that it will be used by God to restore the truth of the resurrection to its proper prominence in our thinking.

I first heard this teaching at a conference for students from St Ebbe's Church, Oxford. We sat in a cold barn with a fierce wind whistling outside but our attention never wandered. We were held not just by the simple clarity and quirky humour of Sam's style, which you will soon appreciate as you read on, but above all by the dynamic power of Christ's resurrection. One student told me afterwards that he had since begun a habit of starting each day by reminding himself that Christ has risen. 'Now that I've been gripped by that truth,' he said, 'I feel like a new man; my understanding of myself, the future and the world I live in have all been completely transformed.'

May God use this book to produce a similar effect in many lives. There is much that could depress us as we read the newspapers or look into our hearts, but those who know that Jesus is alive will always have hope, even in the most depressing circumstances. Jesus Christ is Lord! He has the power to change us now, so that we begin to be the people we long to be. And one day he will return to rid the world of all the ravages of sin.

Christ is risen!

He has risen indeed! Alleluia!

Vaughan Roberts
Easter 2009

Acknowledgments

IN MANY WAYS this has felt like a team project. Eleanor Trotter at IVP has shown cheerful grace and patience with a first-time author who doesn't really know how all this works, and I never realized how awful my grammar was until Mollie Barker sent back the copyedited manuscript with red ink all over it. Thank you both for all your labours.

As with any project like this, I have benefited greatly from the teaching of others. I am particularly grateful for the preaching of John Stott, Phillip Jensen and John Woodhouse. (In fact, I'd better come clean straight away and confess that some of the headings I use in chapter 1 have come from Stott.)

Vaughan Roberts has been a wonderful boss, mentor and friend, and may never know the extent to which his ministry has preserved and encouraged me. Daniel Roe, Joe Clarke, Tim Lewis, Laura Inglis, Michael Jensen and Mark Ellis were all happy to be guinea pigs for this project, and some of them even got round to reading it. God has been generous indeed in giving me friends such as these.

My final thanks need to go to Brian and Leslie Roe of Oak Hill, Virginia for their matchless hospitality during the summer this was written, and to the staff of the nearby Panera coffee shop for eventually getting rid of the squeaky toast machine.

Sam Allberry
May 2009

Introduction

IT WAS DARK AND RAINING and I was late. I was driving through unfamiliar country lanes to visit friends who'd recently moved to this region. According to the route finder I should have arrived some time ago. The road seemed to twist around and fling me about in all sorts of directions I didn't remember noticing on the map when I had set out. I was evidently lost.

Eventually the road took another unexpected turn and plunged me straight into a village whose sign indicated that I'd somehow managed to find my destination. I pulled up against the first building I could find and was about to call my friends to find out where they actually lived, when I realized that I was already right outside their window. I was happy to see them, of course, but even happier to see their spare bed. After a long, cold, damp and tiring journey I wasn't really interested in doing anything other than sleeping.

When I pulled back the curtains the next morning I was amazed. We were high up overlooking a valley whose floor was spread below. Wooded hills stretched in each direction and a river cut its way through the bottom of the valley. The mist hanging over the trees made it feel like somewhere more exotic than Somerset. Down to the left was a beautiful viaduct that I must have passed on my way up the night before. I'd had no idea my friends had moved to such a stunning place. It occurred to me how strange it was that I'd spent so much time in this beautiful scenery the previous night without even realizing it. And yet here it was. It's where I'd been all this time.

Studying what the Bible has to say about the resurrection of Jesus Christ has had a similar effect on me. It has shed light on a Christian landscape that I'd spent so much time in without even realizing it. The contours, twists and turns that I've been navigating for years – sometimes with frustration, sometimes with exhilaration – are now more visible. I can now make sense of them in the light of this extraordinary doctrine. The truth and reality of the resurrection illuminates the detail of so much of our everyday Christian experience.

It occurred to me a couple of years ago that I'd never really heard much teaching on the resurrection that (a) didn't take place on Easter Sunday, or (b) wasn't directed primarily at the sceptic or enquirer. In either case the main focus was attempting to establish the historicity of the resurrection. It is not hard to see why. If we're honest, the resurrection is not always an easy thing to think about. We know (probably) that it matters, and that it matters a great deal. But to those who aren't Christians it can often seem as though the resurrection lacks credibility. And among Christian believers it can often feel as though it lacks relevance. It is a belief we often affirm but rarely consider. It doesn't seem pressing. Lots of other issues feel more immediate and more urgent.

Credibility and relevance – let's consider these briefly.

Problem 1: Credibility

The resurrection on a weekday

Many churches recite the Apostles' Creed as a summary of the Christian faith. It includes this affirmation about the resurrection of Jesus Christ: 'On the third day he rose again . . .' How does it sound?

Imagine it's a Sunday morning. You're in a church service and surrounded by a couple of hundred other Christians. You've been singing of the life-changing presence of Jesus. The minister leads the congregation in a moving, heartfelt prayer of thanks to the risen Christ for his ongoing work in our lives. As you stand you're invited to recite the Creed together, and the words could not be more natural coming off your lips: 'On the third day he rose again . . .' You mean it, with every fibre in your body.

Imagine it's a Monday morning. You're at work grabbing a top-up from the water-cooler and a colleague catches your eye. She knows you're a Christian and makes a couple of comments about how in line she is with Jesus' teaching about loving neighbours. 'He was one of the most amazing teachers,' she says. 'But I don't think he was divine. I don't think he meant us to worship him or anything.' Others listening in nod their approval as if this were the most obvious conclusion. You think back to the words you said about Christ in church yesterday. How do they sound now?

Imagine it's a Saturday evening and you're out with friends. Some have had a bit too much to drink and the talk is now free-flowing. One leans in close to you and just from his breath you know exactly what his last four drinks were. 'You see, once you're dead – that's it. Nothing else. So: enjoy yourself. That's what I think.' The conduct of pretty much everyone else around you seems to confirm that. 'On the third day he rose again' – how does that sound now?

Imagine it's a Wednesday afternoon. It's the funeral of a much-loved relative. It's a humanist service. Your family, eyes red with tears, give you a very clear don't-start-on-that-Christianity-stuff-now look. You gaze across at the coffin and at the mourners gathered round. You hear someone muttering something about how lovely the service was and how it was 'just what she would've wanted'. And those words come back to you again. How do they sound here?

It seemed so natural in church. But like stained glass, pale-green crockery and ineffective heating systems, what seems natural in church can be quite out of place in another context.

Is Jesus like a stuffed tiger?

Until it finished its run in the mid-1990s, one of the world's most popular comic strips was 'Calvin and Hobbes'. Calvin is a six-year-old boy, and Hobbes is his stuffed toy tiger. When others are around, Hobbes is just a toy, but when it's just the two of them Hobbes is real and alive and Calvin's best friend. They can have an adventure together for pages and pages, but as soon as someone else enters the scene Hobbes is just a lifeless toy once again.

Many people think that's how Christian belief works. In your own private context it's real: Jesus is there and he really did rise from the dead. But out in the real world, in the public domain, it's not really true and feels conspicuously unreal. Outside of the Christian context the resurrection seems to lack credibility.

It helps to recognize that this has always been so. Christian belief in the bodily resurrection of Jesus Christ has never seemed credible to society, right from the time of the first believers to the present day. People sometimes say that we can't believe that sort of thing in this day and age, not with what we now know about the world. But it was no less absurd 2,000 years ago. People in the ancient world also knew that dead bodies did not physically rise. It was as counter-intuitive then as it is now. That dead bodies remain dead is not a modern discovery. It wasn't that Christianity arose in an age that was particularly gormless and gullible. Our problem with credibility is not a new one.

The resurrection: 'petty and unworthy'?

That said, we do feel the force of it. Richard Dawkins is one of the most influential atheist writers today. Once, in a debate with a leading Christian scientist, his opponent mentioned the resurrection of Jesus as being a key belief of the Christian faith. This is how Dawkins replied: 'We come down to the resurrection of Jesus. It's so petty. It's so trivial. It's so local. It's so earth-bound. It's so unworthy of the universe.'[1]

This is a sentiment many today would share. Christians, it seems, should feel embarrassed by their belief in the resurrection. If we want Christianity to get anywhere in the world today, we should apparently ditch this kind of belief.

Problem 2: Relevance

And what is the relevance of the resurrection? Some Christians decide to drop it altogether, as if it were a sort of option that you didn't have to sign up to. Some ignore it and many go as far as denying it. This might be one way to respond to the problem, but as we'll see it raises a whole host of more serious questions.

Other Christians, while believing in the resurrection (or at least knowing they're *supposed* to believe in it), are still at a loss to know what to do with it. They tick the box every now and then – if they happen to be in a church where they say the Creed, or if they are being given a particular leadership position and have to sign up to a statement of faith – but then effectively stick it back in a drawer for the rest of the year. We'll take it out on Easter Sunday for its annual dust-off, but it's not really needed apart from that. It's like half the stuff in your garden shed: you know you shouldn't throw it out, but it's not been of any practical use for the last five years.

Two reasons to take it out of the drawer

Two things should make us think twice about this. One is the importance of this belief in Scripture. We'll look at this in due course, but note for now what Paul says: if Christ has not been raised then our faith is futile. It's as simple as that. The resurrection doesn't sound like something which can be left in a drawer for fifty-one weeks of the year. When something matters to the Bible writers and not to us, it's usually a sign that we've got some catching up to do.

> When something matters to the Bible writers and not to us, it's usually a sign that we've got some catching up to do.

The other caution is the importance of this belief in church history. It has been a truth precious to Christians for centuries. It's a good principle for us to follow: if we find ourselves out of sync with the majority of Christians in history then it probably means *we've* missed something, not them. When was the last time you thought about the significance of the Trinity, for example? The resurrection of Christ may not seem important to us, but since when was 'what seems important to us' a sure guide to anything?

For many Christians then the resurrection is a nice thing to believe but not necessarily vital. It's the 'happy ending' to the gospel, or, as one friend put it, the Big Tick after the Big Cross. It's as though, after the dark events surrounding the cross, Steven Spielberg was brought in to do the ending.

We need to think again. The resurrection changes everything. It guarantees our forgiveness, empowers us to change, and gives us a hope for the future and an urgent mission in the present. Four things: assurance, transformation, hope and mission. It is not that we've never experienced them before: in varying degrees they are part and parcel of the daily Christian life. Nor is it the case that once we consider the light the resurrection sheds on them we will always experience them fully and consistently. This side of heaven, we will never be perfectly free from inconsistencies in our behaviour and doubts in our beliefs. But it is the case that understanding the resurrection will transform our appreciation of these four areas of the Christian life, for they properly flow from it. In many cases I suspect we've been living among them without knowing it, experiencing them without realizing that we have them only because 'on the third day he rose again'.

It's where we've been all this time.

1

Assurance

How to shop in your PJs

I'm not a fan of shopping. My tolerance threshold is approximately eighteen minutes. After that I'll buy literally anything if it means I can go home, which explains some of the clothes I wear. And so I approach shopping trips in the same way an SAS team approaches covert missions: identify the target; know where it is; do not deviate to the left or the right; be out of the store before the next customer has even advanced to the counter.

The solution to all this, of course, is online shopping. It is wonderful, for four reasons:

1. You don't have to go outside. No need to face crowds, queues and tempers. You can do it in your pajamas in between Scrabble moves on Facebook.
2. It means you get interesting post. Now that most personal communication is electronic, it tends to be just junk mail and bills that come through the door.

There is nothing to look forward to in the post any more.

3. By the time the package arrives you can't quite remember what you'd bought. It's like someone has sent you a surprise present. And because that 'someone' is you, there is no risk you won't like it. It is me in the past sending gifts ahead to me in the future. It's virtually time travel.

4. You get to sign for stuff. I don't know why this makes me feel significant – it just does. It's something about someone in uniform presenting me with documents needing my signature.

When you think about it, this last point is quite important. If a company or person is sending something of particular value, then it is not enough for them to know that the parcel has been sent: they also need to know it has been received, that it's all gone through and been completed.

Signing off on salvation

The resurrection of Jesus Christ is God signing off on our salvation. It is the proof that sin has been paid for. The payment has been made – we know this because Jesus said his death was going to be a ransom for sin (see Mark 10:45). But we can now know that payment of his blood has been received and accepted: we have God's signature. This is why the true symbol for the Christian faith is an *empty* cross. A crucifix speaks of death, of a payment made. But an empty cross speaks of payment received: 'He was delivered over to death for our sins and was *raised to life* for our justification' (Romans 4:25, my emphasis).

The resurrection means that we can be assured of our salvation. It confirms two things: that Jesus is who he says he is, and that he's done all that he said he would. The Saviour is vindicated in the face of all who rejected his claims. Salvation is assured in the face of all our doubts.

The resurrection assures us of who Jesus is

We need to listen in on what the first Christians had to say. In particular, we need to listen to Peter, who had much to say about the resurrection to anyone who'd listen. We join him in Acts chapter 3. Peter has just healed a beggar, someone who had been crippled from birth and who was well known to many for his prominent begging spot at the entrance to the temple. He would have been there most days. But on this day he didn't get change, but changed. He asked Peter for alms, but received legs!

Needless to say, this healing becomes a sensation. Very quickly, large crowds gather as word spreads. Peter begins to address them. But his focus is not on what has just happened – it's on the resurrection of Jesus, to which the healing of this man points. In the course of his speech Peter gives us a quick three-pointer about Jesus: 'You killed the author of life, but God raised him from the dead. We are witnesses of this' (Acts 3:15).

'You killed him.
God raised him.
We saw him.'

Peter says three crucial things about Jesus that make sense of the time in which his hearers found themselves, and show us exactly what the resurrection means for our salvation. He says, in effect: 'You killed him. God raised him. We saw him.' In other words: condemnation, reversal, public vindication.

'You killed him'

Peter doesn't want the crowds to focus on what *he* had done for the beggar a few moments earlier, but on what *they* had done to Jesus a few *weeks* earlier. 'You killed him,' he says. Here they were, marvelling at the healing that had just taken place. But these were the very same crowds who had bayed for Jesus' crucifixion. In these three words we have, concertina'd together, all the various forms of rejection Jesus faced in the last days and hours of his life. If we were to double-click on this statement the following four components would drop down.

CONDEMNED BY THE JEWS

In the Jewish religious court, Jesus was asked point-blank whether he was the Christ, the Son of the Blessed One. He didn't duck the question, or attempt to side-step it with some nifty footwork. It was a direct question and he gave a direct answer: 'I am.' It was unambiguous.

It also had a kick to it.

The name we give someone to call us by indicates the kind of relationship we want to have with him or her. If I meet a newcomer at my church and tell him he can call me 'Pastor' or 'Reverend', it implies I'm not intending to have a very personal relationship with him: I'm only dealing with him in my capacity as a church leader. It's all very functional. If I tell him to call me 'Mr Allberry', it's a little more personal, but there is still a measure of distance. But if I give him my first name it's all much closer. It's personal. Friendship is on the table.

One of the most precious truths for God's people in the Old Testament was that God had given them his personal name. He had disclosed himself to them personally. They were on first-name terms. It had come about when God asked Moses to lead the Israelites (you can read about this in Exodus 3).

Moses was reluctant for various reasons, one of which was not really knowing how to explain how he knew who God was. And so God gave Moses his card, if you like. The people now had a name by which they could know the God who was leading them. It came to embody the privilege they had in knowing him personally. It became so precious that they avoided speaking and writing it directly. The name? 'The LORD', in our Bibles; but in Hebrew 'Yahweh', literally, 'I am'.

Jesus was doing more than answering the question in the affirmative. He was embodying his answer. He was claiming the divine name for himself. The court didn't need any lengthy deliberations. The high priest spoke for them all when he condemned Jesus to death for blasphemy. And so they handed him over to the Romans.

Executed by the Romans

It was the Romans who sentenced Jesus to death. Pilate may not have regarded all this as anything more than the internal squabbling of the Jewish community. But given the claim of *kingship* being attached to Jesus, it was a squabble that had at least nominally imperial implications. Stability was the order of the day, and yet here was a situation which could potentially cause huge unrest. The crowds were baying for crucifixion. And yet Pilate saw an opportunity for both resolution and political capital. A popular insurrectionist, Barabbas, would be released and Jesus would be executed. The formal charge against him was sedition – he was, after all, claiming to be a king.

Abandoned by God

But Jesus' rejection was not only ecclesiastical and judicial. It was spiritual. In each of the Gospel accounts of the crucifixion of Jesus, the details of his physical sufferings are very sparse.

The whole lengthy and agonizing process is summed up in just three words: 'they crucified him'. We are spared the unpleasant details of what this would have involved. We are not told how Jesus felt at each unbearable stage. But we are told what he *said*. In the thick of the darkness that engulfed the sorry episode, we hear these words being cried out, 'My God, my God, why have you forsaken me?' (Mark 15:34).

We don't need to know the blow-by-blow account of how Jesus' body tore itself apart. What we do need to know is given to us in those words. Jesus is forsaken by God. This takes us to the heart of his death. His suffering was not ultimately physical (hard though that is to conceive), but spiritual: separation from the Father as the Son bore the penalty of our sins. It was as though the Father turned his back on him.

Buried by his disciples

Burial is often the moment of final closure in the grieving process. A week ago I stood with a grieving family as they buried the ashes of their mother. She had actually died several months earlier and had been cremated. Up till now the family had kept the ashes at home. But they felt they hadn't yet fully said goodbye. So they had come to bury them. I led a short service, and as each took a turn to drop a handful of soil down onto the casket, they said their final goodbyes.

The final confirmation of Jesus' rejection is his physical burial. He is laid in the tomb of a prominent politician, Joseph of Arimathea. The body is disposed of. It's the end of the story – a final, all-too-tangible confirmation of those words, 'You killed him'.

'God raised him'

Every other human story has ended at this point. When you get to the corpse being laid to rest, there's no more story to tell. In a biography this is where the final reflection begins, or in a movie where the closing credits start to crawl up the screen. But Peter has only reached the conclusion of his first point, and as we reach for our coats and shuffle to the exit he calls us back with another three words: 'God raised him.' Again, he packs a wealth of information into this short statement. Having thought about the particulars of Jesus' rejection we can begin to make sense of what his resurrection means.

The story of his resurrection is the story of a great reversal – the ultimate reversal. The one who was so roundly condemned is raised to life. On the third day the grave is empty and Jesus is seen. The resurrection vindicates him, and as with his rejection this vindication is just as multifaceted. As we double-click on 'God raised him' we find it reveals and confirms his four-fold identity: the Son of God, the Christ, the Saviour and the Author of life. The resurrection shows Jesus was exactly who he claimed to be.

THE SON OF GOD

The Old Testament looked to the time when God would install his great King, one whose reign would somehow be everlasting. Psalm 2 describes something of his coronation. In the face of international opposition to him, God declares his commitment to his King with the words, 'You are my Son' (Psalm 2:7).

His enthronement would be public, and would confirm his status as the Son of God decisively. Yet the enthronement would not be as people imagined. Listen to what Paul says in connection to this: '[Jesus] . . . through the Spirit of holiness was declared with power to be the Son of God, *by his resurrection from the dead*: Jesus Christ our Lord' (Romans 1:4, my emphasis).

The resurrection powerfully declares Jesus to be the Son of God. What Jesus has claimed before the Jewish court – to be the 'Son of the Blessed One', a claim that would have seemed so laughable as his lifeless body was lifted from the cross – is now demonstrated to be incontrovertibly true. God has raised him. The 'blasphemer' is shown to be right all along.

The Son of God – it means he is worth listening to. He has *the* inside track on God. He is able to speak authoritatively about God. One of the features of his teaching that immediately struck wonder into his listeners was that he spoke as one who had authority (Mark 1:22), unlike the rabbis of the day. The best they could do was quote the great teachers who had gone before, showing off their mastery of the spiritual classics. Not Jesus. He preached without footnotes, as it were. His authority came from himself. He had a unique relationship to God. He was God's man.

There are times when it is hard to live according to this man's teachings. It might be that they rub up too painfully against our own desires and instincts, or against those of someone close to us. We might be tempted to downplay the importance of his words. Many have, after all. But an empty tomb reminds us why we need to take him seriously. His resurrection has powerfully declared Jesus to be the Son of God. It shouts his credentials at us.

The Christ

Peter was the first to preach an Easter sermon. His conclusion was electrifying and, to his hearers, not a little pointed: 'Therefore let all Israel be assured of this: God has made this Jesus, whom you crucified, both Lord and Christ' (Acts 2:36).

It is the resurrection that supports this conclusion. Peter's reasoning is clear and unanswerable. The Christ was to be far greater than great King David. David himself acknowledged this in Psalm 110, to which Peter directs his listeners:

> The Lord said to my Lord:
>   'Sit at my right hand
> until I make your enemies
>   a footstool for your feet.'
> (Acts 2:34–35, quoting Psalm 110:1)

The psalm refers, confusingly to our ears, to two 'Lords'. The first refers to God himself. The second is unidentified in this psalm. All we know is that David is subject to him – 'my Lord'. So David says in effect, 'God said to my Lord: "Sit at my right hand . . . "' This 'Lord', to whom David is subject, is given the place of highest honour by God: to sit at his right hand. This is not some temporary arrangement. He is granted this exalted position, and in the meantime God is going to defeat all his enemies. No rejection of this King will persist. All his enemies will be humiliated before him – a footstool for him. His rule comes from God himself and will ultimately be irresistible. It has divine sanction, and will be universal and enduring. Whoever this figure is, David clearly recognizes his own subordination before him. However great David was (and to those listening to Peter, David was pretty much as good as it got) this figure is greater. He outstrips David on all criteria.

Peter's point is therefore this: David has told us (note, *David* has told us) that there is one greater than he. David's kingship is but a shadow of this definitive King. Yet, since David was the greatest king in Israel's history, this expectation was still to be fulfilled. Israel was still waiting for her true Christ. And that wait is now over. One man has been raised up from death to life, from earth to heaven, exalted at the right hand of God. David's Lord has come, and his rule is now established. The resurrection shows Jesus to be the true Christ, the true King. The man charged with sedition is shown to be the Ruler that God himself has appointed for the whole world.

Jesus may not be popular in the public square. Actually, it was in the public square that his execution was called for. But it is that same public square over which the resurrection shows him to be sovereign.

Western society in many ways doesn't like Jesus – unless he's in a crib, and even then there's a debate. He is like cell phones and cash: not to be flashed about in public. It's fine to believe in him, but you're asking for trouble if you start displaying him where everyone can see him. Keep him to yourself. Stick him in your pocket, and don't take him out till you get home.

The resurrection does not give us that option. He left the grave, not to stand in some discreet corner, but to take his throne in heaven – a throne that is universal and everlasting. He owns and rules the public square. We mustn't keep him indoors, no matter what the neighbours think. He is God's King.

THE SAVIOUR

Those watching the crucifixion of Jesus were well aware of the irony. This man had styled himself as everybody's Saviour. Yet here he was in utter helplessness. And so the jibes came: 'He can't save himself!' What kind of Saviour is that? It was laughable. And yet there is a double irony at work here. For it transpires that he won't save himself *because* he is the Saviour. His crucifixion was to be the means by which he did save others. Had he chosen to save himself, he would have been no Saviour to anybody else.

Back to Peter's preaching – this time a little later, to the Jewish council and high priest: 'The God of our fathers raised Jesus from the dead – whom you had killed by hanging him on a tree. God exalted him to his own right hand as Prince and Saviour that he might give repentance and forgiveness of sins to Israel' (Acts 5:30–31). Jesus is described as having been hung on a tree. In Jewish thought, to be hung on a tree and to be nailed to a cross amounted to pretty much the same thing – the two are synonymous. In fact, describing Jesus as being hung on a tree gives his death extra meaning. In the Old Testament this form of execution was a sign of being under a curse from God.

The manner of his death showed that Jesus was accursed. He was paying for sin. But not his own sin: this death is the means by which forgiveness will come to God's people. Jesus is the Saviour. He became the curse sinners deserved (see 2 Corinthians 5:21). The purpose of his death is indicated by his resurrection. The curse is overturned, Jesus' life is restored. He saves because it is our curse he is bearing.

If we are in any doubt that the cross did its work, the resurrection is where we need to look. There need be no uncertainty. The payment has gone through. His sacrifice has been received and accepted. He really is our Saviour. He didn't come just to teach us and live for us, but to die for us and be raised up for us. Those outrageous claims about his death paying for sin have been proved right. God is holding him up high for everyone to see.

The Author of life

Death is final. When we say goodbye at death we don't expect to say hello again. But not in the case of Jesus – and not in the case of those who follow him (more on that later). In his case the natural processes of death are arrested and Jesus comes through death to new life. Here is Peter, our resurrection tour guide, again: 'You killed the author of life, but God raised him from the dead' (Acts 3:15).

Jesus died. Billions of people have – great leaders and philosophers and teachers among them. But Jesus passed through death, and no-one else has done that. His relationship to life is unique. He is above death; it cannot hold or contain him. His resurrection shows him to be the Author of life.

I've twice moved home in the last few years, and each time into rented accommodation. It is a lengthy process – all that packing up, transportation, unloading, unpacking and gradual distributing. But all of this can only happen because one particular thing has previously been arranged and agreed upon: my receiving the keys from the landlord. Obvious as that is, if it doesn't happen, none of the rest of it is going to achieve anything. I need to know that person, to have sorted everything out with that person and, finally, to have received the keys from that person. The whole process depends on that one part.

All life is his and he owns it. He is the Author of life. If we want to have eternal life then he is the man we need to see.

Peter is telling us that, through his resurrection, Jesus is jingling a bunch of keys before us. The keys to life. All life is his and he owns it. He is the Author of life. If we want to have eternal life then he is the man we need to see. 'I am the resurrection and the life,' he claimed. 'He who believes in me will live, even though he dies' (John 11:25). He holds the keys to it all.

THE BOTTOM LINE

'God raised him.' This is the definitive reversal. It is so much more than another story of a local boy coming good in the end. The so-called blasphemer is in fact the Son of God. The one charged with sedition is the true Ruler. The one under the curse of God is saving others from it. The one buried in a tomb has the power to create life.

The resurrection is an open challenge to how people see Jesus. He cannot be anything less than the Son of God, the Christ, the Saviour, and the Author of life. God has overturned the verdict of humanity on this man, and calls on us to do the same if we haven't already. The resurrection lifts Jesus conclusively out of any merely human category. It defies us to declare our allegiance to him and worship him. Jesus is vindicated.

'We saw him'

Peter's final comment indicates that the vindication of Jesus is public. None of this has happened behind closed doors. It wasn't human sleight of hand or trickery – God did this. And he did it publicly on the stage of human history. It happened, we're told repeatedly, on the third day. Jesus' resurrection was as precise a historical event as his birth or death.

It is worth pausing briefly at this point to reflect that this is the Jesus to whom Christians relate: the man who lived, died and rose again during a particular time in history. The Jesus we know is not some abstract or ahistorical figure. He is not a concept, or even just a meaningful spiritual entity. Jesus is what he is to us precisely *because* he died and rose in human history. We cannot divorce him from these events.

A key demonstration that God has exalted his King is that the risen Jesus was seen by his disciples. He appeared to his followers. We are given accounts of this in each of the four Gospels. In 1 Corinthians 15 Paul itemizes them. There were six occasions when Jesus appeared: to Peter; to the twelve disciples; to a crowd of over 500; to James; to the apostles; and finally to Paul himself. Paul is in no doubt about the importance of these appearances: they form part of the gospel on which believers stand:

> Now, brothers, I want to remind you of the gospel I preached to you, which you received and on which you have taken your stand. By this gospel you are saved, if you hold firmly to the word I preached to you. Otherwise, you have believed in vain.
> (1 Corinthians 15:1–2)

The Jesus in whom we believe died, was buried, rose again and was seen. And what the burial was to his death, the appearances were to his resurrection. The death of Jesus was physically attested by his burial, and his resurrection was physically attested by his appearances. Burial proves he died; being seen proves he rose again.

Some have claimed that these appearances were not real. Maybe the whole idea of the resurrection was triggered by mass hallucinations. Maybe it was auto-suggestion or cognitive dissonance: Jesus' followers so badly wanted him to be raised that they were unable to recognize any evidence to the contrary.

THE DISCIPLES' EXPECTATIONS

These alternative suggestions are not new. Much has been said in response to them, but it is worth noting one key historical fact which they overlook: the disciples were not expecting Jesus to rise again. Each of the Gospels makes this clear. Jesus had predicted his death and resurrection on a number of occasions and yet the disciples had not believed him. After all, on that Easter Sunday morning where were they? They weren't waiting outside the tomb, party-poppers and streamers at the ready for when Jesus emerged. They were pretty much hiding under a table somewhere back in

Jerusalem, terrified that the next knock at the door might be the authorities rounding up the last dregs of the Jesus movement to finish this thing once and for all. When the first women to see the risen Jesus told the other disciples, it was *news* to them. It was not what they had expected. They assumed it was all over. Any hopes they had for the movement Jesus had come to establish had died when he was crucified. They were going to head back home. Maybe the fishing was still good back in Galilee.

Jesus appeared to his disciples and it was a transforming experience. We cannot account for what happened next in history in any other way: they really did see him.

THE DISCIPLES' TRANSFORMATION

We're all used to before-and-after adverts, and in many cases they can lack credibility. The image 'before' someone tries the miracle weight-loss programme or anti-balding treatment is usually suspiciously smudgy, dark and grainy. You're vaguely aware that there's someone there – if only because he's conspicuously overweight or bald – but it's very hard to tell what he looks like. The 'after' picture, by contrast, is crystal-clear and bright, and we can clearly see someone in the peak of health: his body is in great shape, or he has a frankly alarming amount of hair on his head. It's very hard to believe it's really the same person in each picture.

There's no doubt with the disciples, however, just how changed they are by encountering the risen Jesus. The 'before' picture is so *clear*. We see them in the Gospel accounts being consistently slow to understand Jesus. They're not really with him and his agenda. Once the opposition begins to rise in Jerusalem they are easily intimidated and quickly abandon him.

Take Peter, for example. For all his insistence that he will never forsake Jesus, we are given a very detailed account of what finally led him to disown Jesus. An army? Torture? It takes *a servant girl*. She recognizes him as being one of the disciples, and his Galilean accent is also a bit of a give-away. And Peter loses it, insisting even to the point of cursing that he didn't know Jesus. A servant girl. I like to think she had freckles and pigtails. Nice one, Peter.

After the resurrection it is a very different story. We see the spectacular growth of Christianity, propelled by the conviction that the crucified Nazarene is in fact the risen Lord. These same disciples display huge amounts of boldness and determination, often in the face of brutal opposition. And Peter, whose knees trembled before that servant girl, is the first to get on his feet and declare to the Jerusalem crowds that God had made this Jesus both Lord and Christ. There has been a transformation. And Peter accounts for it in those three simple but history-changing words: 'We saw him.' Jesus has been vindicated – publicly. The historical record, presented in the Gospels and in Acts, speaks for itself.

The resurrection demonstrates who Jesus is. It is not meant to be just some mega-miracle, or trump card for the existence of God. It speaks powerfully of the identity of Jesus. We can be assured that he is exactly who he claimed to be. And because of that same resurrection, we can also be assured that he achieved in his death exactly what he had said he would – we can be assured of our salvation. The resurrection compels us to see something of who Jesus is. It also compels us to see something of what he has done.

The resurrection assures us of what Jesus has done

No resurrection = no salvation

'He was delivered over to death for our sins and was raised to life for our justification' (Romans 4:25). This is something of a summary of the gospel Paul has been outlining to his readers in Rome: Jesus was delivered over to death for our sins, and raised to life for our justification. Notice the connection between his resurrection and our justification.

To justify something is to declare it to be right. In an exam we might be challenged to 'justify our answer', in other words, to show it to be right. Paul is speaking of being justified by God: as far as God is concerned, we are entirely in the right. There is nothing to be said against us.

Paul has already shown us that we are justified freely through God's grace as we trust in the death of Jesus. Now he shows us how this justification is related to the resurrection. But let's be clear what Paul doesn't mean. He is not saying that we are half-saved by the cross and half-saved by the resurrection. Rather, Paul is saying that the resurrection is both the consequence and demonstration of salvation through the death of Jesus. His blood saves because he is risen. The resurrection is necessary for justification – without it we are not justified.

Nor are we forgiven. Paul says this in another letter: 'If Christ has not been raised, your faith is futile; you are still in your sins' (1 Corinthians 15:17). Because the death of Jesus has paid for our sins he has been raised to life. Without the resurrection our sin remains unpaid for, and we remain under its dominion. The resurrection is necessary for justification and necessary for salvation.

Why?

Why do we need the resurrection for these things to be certain? Why does the *resurrection*, as opposed to something else, indicate that the death of Jesus has paid for our sins? Presumably God could have yelled down in an audible voice that the sacrifice of Jesus had been accepted. Why is *this* his signature – his signing off on our salvation?

In the logic of Scripture, there is a reason why the resurrection functions in this way. The raising of Jesus from death is significant because death itself is significant. Unless we understand something of the biblical meaning of death, we will not be able to grasp the biblical meaning of resurrection.

The resurrection is the consequence and demonstration of our salvation because death is the consequence and demonstration of our sin.

What we need to see is this: the resurrection is the consequence and demonstration of our salvation because death is the consequence and demonstration of our sin. And to see this we need to go back a bit – in fact back a long way.

Understanding sin

It's Genesis 2. The Garden of Eden. Adam and Eve. God has provided abundantly for the first people. They can enjoy everything they see around them, with one exception. There is one tree they are not to eat from.

> And the LORD God commanded the man, 'You are free to eat from any tree in the garden; but you must not eat from the tree of the knowledge of good and evil, for when you eat of it you will surely die.'
> (Genesis 2:16–17)

The Tree of the Knowledge of Good and Evil. It's a funny name for a tree, but a telling one all the same. It shows us this restriction is not arbitrary. It's not as if God has decided to make one tree out of bounds deliberately, to provoke and test them.

On a shared computer in our church office I once found a file on the desktop marked, 'Do NOT under ANY circumstances open this folder.' I couldn't resist. Once opened it summoned a text which said, 'You're so predictable, and I bet you're a boy!'

Some people think the forbidden tree was similar to this – a kind of trick to prove how helplessly inquisitive we are. Not so. The name is key: The Tree of the Knowledge of Good and Evil. It doesn't mean that to eat of this tree helps Adam and Eve know what right and wrong is, as if they were moral blank sheets up till that point. God had already spelt out to them what they should and shouldn't do. No, to eat from this tree is to have their eyes opened and be *like God*, knowing good and evil. To know it in the way he does.

How does God know good and evil? He knows it as the one who determines and decides it. To eat from this tree is to claim that privilege, to choose to be the one who determines right and wrong. It is an act of rebellion against God, for he alone has the right to show us how to live. As I once heard someone express it, sin is not deciding to *break* the rules, it's deciding to *make* the rules.

We need to understand this. Sin is relational. It is trying to overthrow God. If we don't understand the nature of sin we won't understand God's response to it.

Understanding death

THE PUNISHMENT FOR SIN

Sin leads to death. God said that if humans ate from that tree they would 'surely die'. As we have seen, it was an act of rebellion against God's rule. We cannot go up against God and expect to live, not just because God is bigger and we won't succeed (though he is and we won't), but because God is the life-giver. To turn from him is like sawing off the branch you're sitting on. Sin is a form of suicide, for it cuts us off from the source of our life and breath.

This is seen in what happens to Adam and Eve. The consequence of their sin is that they live under the certainty of death.

> The LORD God made garments of skin for Adam and his wife and clothed them. And the LORD God said, 'The man has now become like one of us, knowing good and evil. He must not be allowed to reach out his hand and take also from the tree of life and eat, and live forever.' So the LORD God banished him from the Garden of Eden to work the ground from which he had been taken. After he drove the man out, he placed on the east side of the Garden of Eden cherubim and a flaming sword flashing back and forth to guard the way to the tree of life.
>
> (Genesis 3:22–24)

They will return to the ground. They are barred from access to the tree of life. Death is inevitable.

THE WAGES OF SIN

This connection between sin and death is reflected elsewhere in the Bible. Paul tells us that 'the wages of sin is death' (Romans 6:23). Death is what sin deserves.

It doesn't quite have the same ring for us today. Our wages tend to be delivered automatically, directly into our bank account. We don't physically handle or touch them. In my first ever job – working weekends in a local coffee shop – I was paid with cash in an envelope at the end of the week. It was so much more tangible. The wages weren't much, but to physically receive them seemed to mean something. It was *there* in my hand – physical recognition that I had actually done that work. I'd earned it. This was my reward and – bar a few cappuccinos spilt down people's shirts – I really deserved it.

Death is just as physical, just as tangible, and just as deserved a wage for our sin. We really did earn this. It is there: an inevitable reminder that our lives, shorn of the goodness and safety of following God's ways, are now finite and ultimately very fleeting.

THE BIRTH-CHILD OF SIN

James shows us graphically how this relationship between sin and death works:

> When tempted, no-one should say, 'God is tempting me.' For God cannot be tempted by evil, nor does he tempt anyone; but each one is tempted when, by his own evil desire, he is dragged away and enticed. Then, after desire has conceived, it gives birth to sin; and sin, when it is full-grown, gives birth to death.
>
> (James 1:13–15)

James is thinking primarily about temptation here, but in the process of doing so reminds us of the seriousness of sin and its relationship to death.

Understanding temptation

WHERE TEMPTATION COMES FROM

James is at pains to show us that we need to look within ourselves for the source of temptation. Temptation is not God's fault; it is ours. It is our own evil desire that entices us and carries us away. It is not ultimately the fault of our peers, parents, schoolteachers or environment. Evil desires find their genesis from within our very hearts. They are not contracted from outside, but bubble up from within.

How temptation works

That's where temptation is from, and James goes on to show us how it works. He takes us on safari. The language is of the hunt: stalking, luring, striking, felling, killing, removing and devouring. Images from a hundred natural history programmes spill into our minds: a happy group of wildebeest skipping playfully in the savannah, quite oblivious to any danger. Cut to a lioness, crawling stealthily through the tall grass. The wildebeest suddenly look around, sensing something. There's a pounce, a moment or so of struggle, and then it's all over.

So it is with our sinful desires, says James. They are ruthless hunters. Sin is not a force to be underestimated. Yet how often, in the moment of temptation, we assume we're in control, that we can handle it and that we know what we're doing. To play around with sinful desires is to dangle ourselves before a great predator, like two wildebeest teenagers playing chicken near a family of hungry lions.

Sinful desire is also seductive. Think of those predators whose energies go into making themselves attractive to their prey, so that their victims actually deliver themselves up for the taking.

Let's put these two points together: the origin of temptation and the mechanism of temptation. Its origin is us: it is of us/from us/out of our own selves. Yet at the same time it is alien to us: the verbs used by James are passive – we're dragged and enticed as if by something 'other'. And that's the rub: in our fallenness our experience of ourselves is no longer authentic. We experience a tension, in that the 'us' that seems to operate the controls is not the 'us' we sense we ought to be. The 'me' that contrives sin is both me, and yet not me. I have become self-alienated, hijacked by a form of me that is not authentic. There is a contradiction in my very self.

WHERE TEMPTATION LEADS

James tells us what happens next and it gets even worse. We've been enticed and dragged away. The next thing that happens is that desire conceives. Once we succumb, sinful desire gives birth to sinful action (verse 15). The sin that is birthed grows quickly and then itself gives birth to death. The whole sorry process reaches its conclusion.

I have friends who have experienced the painful tragedy of giving birth to a stillborn child. It is a horrific experience and one I'm hesitant even to mention. But it is the image James selects to make his point, and it is proper that it is so horrific. Sin gives birth to death.

What all these passages have in common is that they highlight the relationship between sin and death. Death is the punishment, wages and birth-child of sin.

DEATH THE INTRUDER

I think this is why we have a strange perception of death. It puzzles us. Death is, when we think about it, one of the most normal things about life in this world: it is finite and it ends. This happens to everyone. It's not unusual, and when it happens to people sufficiently far removed from us we can even manage to be indifferent to it. But for all its common-ality, close up, death never seems natural. It seems *wrong*, something that shouldn't really belong to human experience – an unwelcome intruder in our world. And as much as we cover it with euphemisms – a loved one has 'passed away', or 'moved on', or 'left us' – it is deeply uncomfortable for us even to think about. And so we don't. The best we can do is not think about it, pretend it isn't there, live as though it's not going to happen. We don't welcome being reminded that we will all have to face it one day.

Our unease with death is a reflection that we know more than we realize. Death, like sin, does not belong here. Sin leads to death. The existence of death proves the reality of sin. It is the consequence and demonstration that we have sinned against God. It is something we were never intended to experience.

Understanding resurrection

As we grasp the significance of death we can begin to see the significance of resurrection. Raising Jesus from the dead was not an arbitrary power-miracle. It has meaning. The death Jesus dies is a result of sin, yours and mine. The proof that he has paid for sin in full is his resurrection, his coming to new life.

New life, notice. I once heard of a missionary working in Thailand who gave a Buddhist friend of his a New Testament to read through and think about. Some time later when they next met, he was confused to discover that his friend had concluded from doing so that Jesus was an exemplary Buddhist. It took the missionary a long time to work out how someone could draw this conclusion from reading through the four Gospels. But it eventually dawned on him. The Buddhist had read the Gospels through, assuming they were sequential, not parallel, accounts of Jesus. He read each as if it was the next incarnation, and was therefore impressed that after merely four incarnations Jesus had achieved nirvana. He'd finally broken out of this cycle of reincarnation and death, and left this world.

The life Jesus was raised to was not the same kind of life he'd lived before his death, as if he was about to go through the process again. Resurrection is being raised to new life, not normal life. As we shall see later, Jesus' post-resurrection body was radically different from his pre-resurrection body (even if there was also some continuity). His new life shows us that the cycle of sin and death in which we naturally live has finally been broken. He has triumphed over sin once and for all. It is a victory over sin and its consequence that is definitive, not temporary. There is new life to be had. Sin has been conquered.

It is therefore the resurrection of Jesus, and *can* only be the resurrection of Jesus, that assures us of salvation. It is the sign that Jesus has achieved for us all that he claimed he would. Only the resurrection can show us that our sins have been fully dealt with, and that death is now no longer our destination, but a gateway to new and perfect life.

The resurrection shows us that there is nothing we need to add to the death of Jesus to find acceptance with God. The cross is not a starter pack. It is not God drumming up even most of what we need so that we can fish around in our pockets and make up the rest. By dying and rising for us Jesus has closed the deal. God has signed for it, and his signature is the resurrection.

2

Transformation

How to keep your resolutions while breaking them

I have a love–hate relationship with New Year's resolutions.

In the autumn I love them. I love to think about them, and spend weeks looking forward to all the exciting ways in which my life is going to improve – next year I'm going to be healthier! a better cook! more informed! And I love unveiling my resolutions to an eager public come the first day of January.

A few days into the New Year I start to feel a little differently. I begin to realize that keeping resolutions is actually going to involve having to do something. And it just takes a few days' lapse for the much-lauded fresh start to come to a sputtering halt. And those resolutions, which up till then had been beacons of hope and transformation, now sit there looking at me contemptuously.

Around mid-January I start to take a sudden interest in postmodern interpretation. I am reminded that language is fluid. Meaning is a moving target that won't sit still long enough for me to get a firm grip on it. The 'me' who made those resolutions belongs to a different time – indeed, to a different year. I was younger then. The world has changed. My resolutions are now re-examined in the light of this important information. They can be interpreted a little differently – re-understood, if you will. 'Have more fruit' need not necessarily mean 'eat more fruit'. It could mean 'buy more fruit'. So I am now the proud owner of a bowl of gradually rotting oranges and bananas. 'Go to the gym more often' – well, the phrase 'more often' is gloriously vague. In any case, we discover on closer inspection that the gym has a rather pleasant steam room. Job done.

So I start to like New Year's resolutions again. They've been a resounding success. And as the months begin to pass, it occurs to me that I should probably eat more healthily and take more exercise. I get excited about the prospect of introducing these as resolutions for the coming New Year. It'll be a wonderful new start. I'm looking forward to it already.

We want to change.

It seems to be a feature of being human. Maybe not all of us, all the time, in the same way and to the same extent, but virtually all of us, most of the time and to a significant extent, want to be different.

But another feature of being human is that the power to change seems to elude us. Sometimes we can achieve a measure of success here and there. We can become a degree or two nicer or healthier or cleverer. But deep down it's still the same us. And deep down I know that what needs to change in my life is what is deep down. As someone once said, 'Every time we turn over a new leaf we find ourselves on the same page.' When the dust has settled from the grand relaunch of 'me', it turns out that it's just the packaging that's changed.

This desire to change is no different for Christians. In fact we should sense it more than anyone else. Our exposure to God's Word has shown us what we're really made of. We have far more than a hunch to go on that we've not been doing a very good job of being human. God has told us. In the death of Jesus he's shown us just how serious a problem it's been. It turns out we'd massively underestimated what needed to be done. Things were worse than I thought – much worse. My life doesn't need lots of little improvements, like straightening the pictures on the wall or fluffing up the cushions on the sofa. It needs complete renovation. I want to change.

Resurrection now and later

So we need to look at the resurrection. It has implications for us. The Christian is not just someone who 'votes Jesus' from afar. By faith in Jesus we are joined to him and have union with Christ. We are bound up with him, united to him in his death and united to him in his resurrection. Paul, for example, can say that we have 'died with Christ' and been 'raised with Christ'. Christ's fortunes are our fortunes. We are inextricably linked now. His resurrection means our resurrection, and that means change.

It happens in two stages. We are *spiritually* raised now. And we will be *physically* raised at the end of time. So Paul can say to the Colossian Christians, 'Since, then, you have been raised with Christ . . .' (Colossians 3:1). Our spiritual resurrection has taken place already. We put it in the past tense. Our union with Christ means that we have already experienced something of his resurrection.

The most common way Christians are described in the New Testament is as those who are 'in Christ'. One Sunday a mother was showing off her newborn baby at church when someone mentioned that it was the baby's first time at a service. The mother replied, 'Where do you think he's been the past nine months!?' Being in Christ means we go where he goes. He has been raised up to the right hand of God, and as those united to him by faith we have been 'raised with him'.

But we still await our physical resurrection. Paul describes it as 'the redemption of our bodies' (Romans 8:23) and it belongs to the future. We'll come back to that in the next chapter, but for now we need to examine what it means for us to have been raised spiritually with Christ.

We need to recognize something important about God.

The God who brings new life

God's calling card

Summing up people is hard. When we know someone well, it can be hard to pin down exactly what makes them *them*. There are too many things to mention, or so much that it is hard to sum up in just a few words.

Summing up God is harder. He's bigger for a start, not just in size and power, but in terms of his character and nature. Where would you begin? There's no one sentence that would seem to do him justice. None will hit the spot exactly. But there are some verses in the Bible that get us pretty close, and while not exhaustive, they nevertheless take us to the heart of what God is like. One such is Romans 4:17, where Paul describes him as, 'the God who gives life to the dead and calls things that are not as though they were'.

This is the kind of God who is there. Not the God of popular imagination, or of jokes or cartoons. I'd even suggest that this is not the God people don't believe in. This God is far more interesting.

According to this verse he is distinguished by two things: he gives life to the dead, and he calls things that are not as though they were. It might not have been the job description we would have written for him, but think about it for a moment. There are some people who can look at a dismal situation and see not what is there, but what *could* be there. They end up being the kind of people who renovate dilapidated old barns and transform them into exclusive country getaways, or who take over failing companies and turn them around into market leaders. It doesn't need to be said that they get paid a lot of money for this ability. And yet it doesn't come close to what God does.

God takes situations and people that are not just challenging, but actually impossible to turn around. He looks at things that are *not*, not things that are *not quite*, and calls them as though they *were* – and *are* – because in his hands that is what they are going to be.

You might think that Paul has concluded this because of the resurrection of Jesus. It would be natural enough to have done so. But he's actually describing the God in whom Abraham believed. Transformation has always been a feature of God's work. Paul learnt it from the Old Testament. There we discover the God who brings new life. The resurrection of Jesus was not the first time we'd seen God's signature, even if it was the most glorious.

New life from nothing

We see it in the biblical account of creation. God breathes life into the dust, and human life is formed (Genesis 2:7). Life comes from God. It didn't fluke itself into existence. God creates and produces it.

I recently found this definition of atheism on the internet:

The belief that there was nothing and nothing happened to nothing and then nothing magically exploded for no reason, creating everything, and then a bunch of everything magically rearranged itself for no reason whatsoever into self-replicating bits which then turned into dinosaurs.[1]

Genesis introduces us to a pattern that is going to become familiar through the pages of the Bible: God bringing life from non-life.

New life from old people

We see it in creation. We also see it in biblical history. God promises Abraham that he will be the father of a great nation. God points to the stars, tells Abraham to count them, and says to him, 'So shall your offspring be' (Genesis 15:5). Let's remember that Abraham didn't have our problem of light pollution. He didn't live on the edge of London or New York and therefore God wasn't promising him a grand total of just three children. If you've ever been far into the wilderness and seen the stars on a clear night, then you'll know the kind of thing Abraham would have seen. It would have been a sky lit up with stars, blazing with them, many twinkling brightly, patches of dense clusters here and there, and the smear of downtown Milky Way comprising millions and millions more. 'So shall your offspring be.' Abraham is going to be the father of a seemingly countless dynasty.

But there are two problems. First, Abraham is old. Paul puts it at 'about a hundred years old', and if that isn't indelicate enough, he also points out that Abraham's body was 'as good as dead'! Second problem: Abraham's wife Sarah is unable to have children. Actually, Paul doesn't mince his words here either: 'Sarah's womb was also dead' (Romans 4:19). A dead body and a dead womb – not exactly the basis on which to buy a seven-seater family car. We're not talking difficult, but impossible. In fact both of them have a good laugh at the whole idea. We might sympathize with them. But then the idea of God bringing life from death has a long history of being sneered at. Ours is not the first generation to find the idea absurd.

But this is the God who gives life to the dead and calls things that are not as though they were. He knows what he's doing. He's not hampered by the physical limitations of Abraham and Sarah. It's actually the point: the life that comes from this is going to be miraculous and so we'd better get used to the idea. God has said it and so it's going to happen. In time Abraham and Sarah do in fact have a bouncing baby boy.

A dead body and a dead womb – not exactly the basis on which to buy a seven-seater family car. We're not talking difficult, but impossible.

They call him Isaac, which means 'he laughs'. Sarah explains the thinking behind the name: 'God has brought me laughter, and everyone who hears about this will laugh with me' (Genesis 21:6). She had laughed in mockery when God made the promise; now she laughs in joy at its fulfilment. History is littered with people who chuckled at the preposterous notion of God giving life to the dead, but who then came to laugh with pleasure at that new life once it was received.

Sarah's experience is not unique. Elsewhere in the Old Testament, Hannah too is an unhappily childless woman who subsequently enjoys motherhood. Though no doubt deprived of sleep and surrounded by dirty nappies, she sings a song about it, concluding,

> The LORD brings death and makes alive;
>   he brings down to the grave and raises up.
> (1 Samuel 2:6)

Life from no life. Barrenness to vibrant fertility.

New life for a dead nation

It's an image that is even applied to God's people as a nation later in the Old Testament. By this stage they had been disobeying God for generation after generation, and had invited the punishment he had always said would come.

The nation was divided into two rival kingdoms. Israel, the northern part, was conquered by the Assyrians. Then in 587 BC the Babylonian war machine trundled over the border of Judah, the southern part, and the nation crumbled.

The capital city Jerusalem, and the spiritual security it had come to represent, was destroyed. Many of those lucky enough to survive were taken captive and deported to far-flung Babylon to live in exile.

It is in this context and at this time that the prophet Ezekiel is given an extraordinary vision by God. He sees before him a valley of dry bones (you can read about it in Ezekiel 37:1–14). The scene is utterly desolate. We can imagine the scorching wind, the valley floor bleached white and Ezekiel stepping carefully as he tries not to crunch the bones underfoot. In this odd setting God gives him a job to do: he's to preach to the bones, so that God will make them live. (If you've read Ezekiel chapters 1 to 36 you'll know that God had already asked Ezekiel to do some pretty strange things, and so he just gets on with it and delivers his sermon.)

As he preaches, strange noises can be heard. Not a stifled yawn or people shuffling uncomfortably in their seats, but the sound of rattling. And in what looks like a scene from a fantasy movie, the bones become animated and covered by layers of tendon, muscle, flesh and skin. Life is breathed into them and they stand before Ezekiel as a vast army.

This isn't just a strange story, or yet another cutting for Ezekiel's scrapbook, or some impressive CGI. It's a lesson, and God explains to him what it means:

Son of Man, these bones are the whole house of Israel. They say, 'Our bones are dried up and our hope is gone; we are cut off.' Therefore prophesy and say to them: 'This is what the Sovereign LORD says: O my people, I am going to open your graves and bring you up from them; I will bring you back to the land of Israel.'
(Ezekiel 37:11–12)

To the spiritually dead there is the promise of life: the prospect of graves emptying, a mass raising up of people as they are spiritually restored. For the nation: life from non-life.

New life that will never end

Within this wider framework the promise of new life is applied to one special individual in particular: King David. The king in Israel was far more than a senior politician. The hopes of the nation and the purposes of God for it were all summed up in this one figure. His authority was not just political but spiritual. He was something of a barometer for the spiritual fortunes of the people as a whole. The progress of a good king had massive benefits for the spiritual well-being of the nation, just as the disobedience and wickedness of an evil king was a disaster that dragged everybody else down.

David was conscious of this significance. He knew the purposes of God that were attached to his office. The king was God's anointed – God's 'Christ'. Throughout David's psalms we find an awareness that the office, and the expectation it represented, was far greater than he was, and that though he was a man after God's own heart and one of Israel's greatest kings, he couldn't hope to fill the shoes of this role. David knew what it meant to be the Christ, and that it ultimately transcended his own experience and achievements. His psalms would occasionally look beyond himself to an ultimate Christ figure who was yet to emerge, the definitive answer of God to the needs of his people.

One promise attached to this ultimate Christ, as David understood it, was that he would not be defeated by death. David describes this Christ figure as saying to God,

> You will not abandon me to the grave,
>   nor will you let your Holy One see decay.
> (Psalm 16:10)

The fact is that David did die. As Peter was to point out to the Jerusalem crowd some time after the resurrection, you could go and visit David's tomb. If you wanted proof that David, Israel's greatest king, was not the ultimate Christ, you just needed to go to the local tourist information bureau and pick up a leaflet all about the tomb and where to find it. Just follow the tour buses. David was not the real Christ, for the real Christ would be victorious even over death.

Life from non-life. Barren wombs, barren people, barren soil, even barren nations – all of them brought to new life by God. It's his signature work, and it doesn't stop at the end of the Old Testament. It reaches a climax with the resurrection of Jesus, and yet it doesn't even stop there. For if we turn to this Christ in repentance and faith, we find ourselves united to him, and in him we ourselves are raised to new life.

New life that transforms us, bringing change that doesn't need to wait till the New Year, and which will long outlast it.

The people who receive new life

The Bible's 'Swoosh'
One of the most famous symbols in the world is the Nike 'Swoosh'. It was designed in 1971 by Carolyn Davidson and

bought by Nike for a princely $35. It's been a hit ever since. Nike takes its name from the Greek goddess of victory, and the smooth upward 'tick' captures this sense of dynamic success. It's a great image for a sportswear company. It also happens to capture brilliantly the shape of God's work through the Bible.

We've seen the biblical Swoosh throughout the Old Testament. God takes dead people and hopeless situations and imparts new life and hope. He is the God who brings life from non-life. While this shape is seen again and again in the Old Testament, it's in the New that it comes in its boldest, most definitive form – in the life, death and resurrection of Christ. We see this shape in Paul's famous description of Christ's ministry:

> Christ Jesus . . .
>   being in very nature God,
>   did not consider equality with God something to be grasped,
>   but made himself nothing,
>   taking the very nature of a servant,
>   being made in human likeness.
>   And being found in appearance as a man,
>   he humbled himself
>   and became obedient to death – even death on a cross!
>   Therefore God exalted him to the highest place
>   and gave him the name that is above every name,
>   that at the name of Jesus every knee should bow,
>   in heaven and on earth and under the earth,
>   and every tongue confess that Jesus Christ is Lord,
>   to the glory of God the Father.
>   (Philippians 2:5–11)

Christ in his humility comes to this world as a servant and suffers the ultimate humiliation of death by crucifixion. It is the ultimate descent: from the glories of heaven to humble human service on earth, and then down further to the alienation and shame of the cross. God's response to this is to exalt him: '*Therefore* God exalted him to the highest place' (my emphasis). Christ is raised to the highest place and given the highest name. It is the ultimate Swoosh. The new-life shape we've seen repeatedly in Scripture beforehand has been a prefiguring, an anticipation of this definitive act of new life by God. What was pencilled-in through the Old Testament has been inked-over in Jesus' death and resurrection.

Yet amazingly God applies this work to us today. As those who trust in Christ we become caught up in this great work of God. Through faith we become united to Christ, joined to him in such a way that his death becomes our death (we died in him), and also so that his life becomes our life (we are raised in him). God's work in us has the same shape as God's work in Christ. He gives us new, resurrection life. The Swoosh is applied to us. With it we enjoy a whole host of newness: new life, new perspective, new conduct, new power and new ambition. Resurrection life changes everything.

New life

It is always interesting to hear stories of how people have come to put their trust in Christ. Sooner or later it's something most Christians will be asked to explain, both by believers and non-believers. It's a good thing to think through, and as we do we become conscious of some of the key turning points: maybe a particular situation we were facing, or a highly significant conversation, or individual, or sermon. As we look back, we might think of particular stages in our becoming Christians, and points we would need to cover in any account of the whole process.

In Ephesians 2, Paul does things a little differently: he gives his friends in Ephesus *their* testimony. He reminds them of how they came to be followers of Christ. And there are two points Paul wants to cover as he reminds them of how it all happened: they were dead in sins, and then they were raised in Christ.

DEAD IN SINS

As for you, you were dead in your transgressions and sins, in which you used to live when you followed the ways of this world and of the ruler of the kingdom of the air, the spirit who is now at work in those who are disobedient. All of us also lived among them at one time, gratifying the cravings of our sinful nature and following its desires and thoughts. (Ephesians 2:1–3a)

That was them to start with: spiritually dead. Three things were bound up with this death: the unholy trinity of the world, the devil and the flesh, a three-fold cord binding them in hopeless disobedience. If we have eyes to see it, here is also a description of us in our natural state. Paul is able to recognize himself in there. 'Like the rest, we were by nature objects of wrath' (Ephesians 2:3b). This is the default condition of humankind. It is where we are and where we remain if left to our own devices. Spiritually dead. Physically we are alive, and in our prime we may even be physically powerful. We certainly don't look dead, but we are. Like characters from a zombie movie we are walking corpses.

If we haven't done so already, we really need to come to terms with this. It is reality, whether we like it or not. In this state God does not look on us with pleasure. We are objects of wrath: tragic and twisted versions of who he made us to be. We are recognizably us, and yet at the same time dreadfully disfigured by sin. Sadly this is of our own making, as we comply with the agenda of those three forces bearing down on us.

As those who were 'dead', there was nothing we could do about it. Our prospects for spiritual life were as promising as those of a bit of road-kill for physical life. Just as a rabbit or fox lying on the pavement with tire marks across its front isn't able to do much to improve its situation, so too we were unable to help ourselves. In such a state, morality is not going to help, nor is our best religious behaviour.

Death here is not a metaphor of something less bad. We were not like the movie hero who, just before the climax, is staggering around with a chest full of bullets, and yet in just a moment is about to dust himself off and pull himself together for the final showdown. We were *dead*, not dead-like or nearly dead, but *really* dead. Dead in our sins.

Then God did something.

Raised with Christ

'Because of his great love for us, God, who is rich in mercy, made us alive with Christ even when we were dead in transgressions – it is by grace you have been saved' (Ephesians 2:4–5). Hear that? Dead, and then made alive. We can almost hear the sound of a Swoosh. God made us alive.

Paul continues the story: 'And God raised us up with Christ and seated us with him in the heavenly realms in Christ Jesus' (Ephesians 2:6). Made alive and raised up – and this dramatic reversal is due entirely to God's love and mercy. We are saved by grace. And only by grace.

Grace is undeserved kindness. A tiny example would be when you're waiting to pull out onto a busy road, and you can feel yourself physically ageing as the constant stream of traffic zooms by. And then someone slows down and signals you in. Just a little gesture and yet it can lift the mood immediately. That is grace. The driver hadn't checked you out first to establish whether you deserved it. He just decided to let you through. Undeserved kindness.

If we take that, magnify it a billion-fold and then double it, we might begin to get a sense of the dimensions of the grace of God in Christ. It wasn't because of anything in us. It wasn't that God thought we would make potentially wonderful Christians, or that he couldn't possibly imagine the gospel cause advancing without having us on the team. It is all undeserved, hence Paul insists in the next couple of verses that we have nothing to boast about.

After we come to Christ, receiving new life, we don't brag about how clever we were in becoming Christians as if it were somehow a reflection of our superior intelligence. If we truly grasp this idea of grace then, stunned that God would do such a thing for us, we could only open our mouths to boast about Christ. It is all from God. If we were dead and are now alive then how could it be anything else? Who else can do that? Dead in sins, now raised in Christ: we have new life. Swoosh!

New perspective

Being raised with Christ means that things are going to start looking a little different. Our perspective will begin to change: our hearts and minds will become set on something new.

> Since, then, you have been raised with Christ, set your hearts on things above, where Christ is seated at the right hand of God. Set your minds on things above, not on earthly things. For you died, and your life is now hidden with Christ in God. When Christ, who is your life, appears, then you also will appear with him in glory.
>
> (Colossians 3:1–4)

Notice the connection: it is because we've been raised with Christ that we need to set our hearts and minds on things above. Our new perspective is mandated precisely because we now experience resurrection life.

UPGRADES AND WEDDING RINGS

I took a transatlantic flight recently and for the first time in my life managed to get an upgrade to first class. (It's all about the jacket.) My first reaction was extreme excitement. I'm not a fan of flying at the best of times – it's something to do with being so crammed into the seat that you can practically lick your knees. So now I could look forward to some comfort and pampering.

As we boarded, I tried to hide my never-done-this-before excitement and instead give the impression that I was accustomed to this sort of thing. Although it wasn't my scene and I hadn't paid for it, it didn't take long into the flight before I began to feel like this *was* my style. I started to feel as though I had paid for it and did deserve it, that it was my birthright. It began to affect how I reacted to any tiny mistake made by the air stewards. My perspective had changed, and not in a particularly good way.

Being raised with Christ should change our perspective. We need to see reality in the light of where we now are. Things are different in resurrection life. We are not where we were, and we need to keep up with that. We need to set our hearts and minds on things above. Notice that it will take some determination on our part. It's not automatic. This new perspective doesn't just 'happen'. Effort is involved. We need resolve: I have been raised with Christ, and I need to keep that in my consciousness. I need to have the concerns and the mindset of a spiritually raised person.

It's a bit like a newly married man. Now this is one of the

things where, in general terms, men and women can be really quite different. In pastoral ministry I get to see many couples go through engagement into marriage, and in my experience at least something of a pattern has begun to emerge.

For the woman (generally), now being a wife changes how she sees *everything*. It's as though she's looking at reality through the lens of her wedding ring. She is *married* now.

With the guys (generally) it tends to be a little different. Blokes tend to be a little more functional, by and large. So while a man's wedding ring is definitely a new and unmistakable part of his mental scenery, it's not necessarily the frame round the whole thing. It's not that it's unimportant, it's just not all-consuming. It's possible for him to see other things and not be always conscious of it. A newly-wed guy might spend many moments without being conscious that he is now a husband. Time might pass in the office before, looking down, he notices his ring and smiles to himself: *I'm married*. He can actually forget it. And so a man like this needs to actually make an effort to think and feel like a married man. It won't always come easily or quickly. His life has changed, and he needs to deliberately think through what that's going to *mean*.

So too with the raised, forgiven sinner. You've been raised with Christ, says Paul. You can't just stick it in your back pocket and get back to business as usual. Put your heart and mind to work. Think like a risen person. What are the new concerns going to be? The new priorities? We have a new perspective. At the very least it's going to spill out into our behaviour.

New conduct

RIGHT PLACE, WRONG CLOTHES

I have a small number of recurring dreams. One involves intruders in the home in the middle of the night, and my attempts to escape. Getting out of the house is normally fine: I slip through the window and get down to the street undetected. The problem is then trying to run away. It's like running through molasses. Try as I might, I'm unable to move forward at anything above a pathetic speed. Glaciers could overtake me. At some point during this fruitless attempt to move forward, all the while waiting for my assailants to pounce, I wake up in a cold sweat, and wonder why the bedding is all over the floor.

One of the other dreams comes less frequently for me, but is experienced by most people at some point. In fact it's a classic. In its childhood setting it's when you turn up at school. For adults it's when you walk into the office, or are about to deliver an important presentation, or begin the difficult meeting, or as you start to teach your class, or (in my case) step up before the congregation to begin the service. That's when everyone notices and the awful realization dawns upon you: you're still in your nightclothes. And as impressive as the *Simpsons* boxers might be in your own mind, this is not the context to introduce them to others.

Resurrection living means a new start has begun for us. The spiritual day has dawned.

It's associated with anxiety, often about new starts: maybe a new term looming, or an event at work, or a placement. In this light it's entirely understandable, even if we feel a little silly about it once we've woken up. Our subconscious is really quite gullible. This sort of thing would never happen. You don't go to work in your sleep clothes, and you don't go to sleep in your work clothes (well, not very often anyway).

But when it comes to resurrection living it's very easily done. In day-to-day life, we have our morning ritual, our own way of making the transition from night-time to day-time. Coffee. Shower. Clothes. Breakfast. (In whichever order you prefer.) Each of us figures this out as soon as we're able. And we need to learn to do it again. Resurrection living means a new start has begun for us. The spiritual day has dawned. As Paul says to the Ephesian Christians,

> For you were once darkness, but now you are light in the Lord . . . Have nothing to do with the fruitless deeds of darkness, but rather expose them. For it is shameful even to mention what the disobedient do in secret. But everything exposed by the light becomes visible, for it is light that makes everything visible. That is why it is said:
>
> 'Wake up, O sleeper,
>   rise from the dead,
>   and Christ will shine on you.'
> (Ephesians 5:8, 11–14)

WAKING IN CHRIST

We've moved from darkness to light, from sleep to being awake, from spiritual death to life in Christ. We've come out of the night of sin and into the new day of life with Christ. The gospel of the death of Jesus has acted as an alarm clock. His word has broken through our slumber and into our consciousness. We're now up: sunlight is streaming through the curtains, birds are chirping outside the window. So now it's time to get dressed. To neglect to do this – to head into the day of resurrection life without having changed our clothes – is like striding into the boss's office still wearing pajamas.

Resurrection means new conduct. I'll let Paul explain:

> Put to death, therefore, whatever belongs to your earthly nature . . . you must rid yourselves of all such things as these: anger, rage, malice, slander and filthy language from your lips. Do not lie to each other, since you have taken off your old self with its practices and have put on the new self, which is being renewed in knowledge in the image of its Creator. (Colossians 3:5, 8–10)

Notice Paul's thinking. The word 'therefore' at the beginning matters: it connects what Paul is saying with what he's just said. *Because* we've been raised with Christ we need to change our conduct. And it involves getting changed: taking off one thing and putting on something else (just in case you didn't know what getting changed meant). What comes off is whatever belongs to our earthly nature, all that characterized life without regard for God. Resurrection means that things have to go. We used to live for other things and our behaviour expressed that. We lived for our own satisfaction and so we were greedy. We lived for the approval of others and so we joined in their impurity. We lived for acceptance and so we lived lives of sexual promiscuity. We have now been raised with Christ – we live for *him*, and our behaviour needs to reflect that.

What we are to put on is the character of Jesus. We're raised with him, seated with him, hidden with him. He is our life, and his character is to be our character. We put him on. We thought too much of ourselves, now we are to be clothed with humility and kindness. We lived for ourselves, now we are to give of ourselves to others. We really are raised with Christ, and we need to behave the part. Christians should be different.

A history tutor commented to me one day that his colleagues in the department could tell who the Christian students were. It wasn't that they wore sandals or had bad breath. It was their character. They were respectful. They handed their papers in on time. They were interested in their subject and applied themselves to it. Those raised with Christ should be different. Our behavioural 'clothes' should stand out a mile. We should be characterized by new conduct.

THE RESURRECTION AND GENEROSITY

We find a powerful example of this new conduct in the book of Acts. In the very early days of the new Christian movement we're given a thumbnail sketch of the fledgling church community.

> All the believers were one in heart and mind. No-one claimed that any of his possessions was his own, but they shared everything they had . . . There were no needy persons among them. For from time to time those who owned lands or houses sold them, brought the money from the sales and put it at the apostles' feet, and it was distributed to anyone as he had need. (Acts 4:32–35)

It's an amazing picture. We know that by this stage the number of believers exceeded 5,000, and yet Luke can narrate that there were no needy people among them. It wasn't a kind of proto-communism: people still had possessions, but they held loose to them and there seemed to be a culture of sharing, of pooling resources.

And not just the small stuff either. They sold their *land*, so as to provide for the needy. Land at that time was the equivalent of the savings portfolio. Land was wealth. And yet there it went, into the pot to help others. Notice too that it is laid at the apostles' feet, for them to distribute. The benefactors did not earmark it for particular uses, or add stipulations and conditions as to how the money might be used. They gave it to the apostles. It wasn't a form of power-by-vast-donation.

We pause to think about this mindset because it is so different from our own. 'The believers were one in heart and mind,' Luke tells us. And this is what it looked like in practice. Their oneness was expressed through their sharing.

But the real reason we need to take in this scene is that Luke wants us to see what empowered that generosity. We missed out a verse in the middle of the quotation above. Here it is again, with that verse added in:

> All the believers were one in heart and mind. No-one claimed that any of his possessions was his own, but they shared everything they had. *With great power the apostles continued to testify to the resurrection of the Lord Jesus, and much grace was upon them all.* There were no needy persons among them. For from time to time those who owned lands or houses sold them, brought the money from the sales and put it at the apostles' feet, and it was distributed to anyone as he had need. (Acts 4:32–35, my emphasis)

Luke inserts this comment about the apostles' preaching into the middle of his account about the early church's giving to make a point. The fuel for their generosity was this message about the resurrection. That is what they were preaching: 'the resurrection of the Lord Jesus'. The result: 'much grace was upon them all'. The resurrection changed their perspective about their wealth and about other Christian people. This new life we live through being raised with Christ is one that is lived in community. I am not an isolated, spiritually raised person. I am united with the risen Christ and with all others who are raised with him. We are knitted to Christ. We are also knitted to one another. And that changes our conduct.

Think about what you own. Think about the Christian community to which you may belong. Do you know them well enough to know their needs? If not, then start. If you do, think about what you own again. How could it be used to help them? But we have more to offer than our possessions. What about time? Or skills? Or a listening ear? How could they all be used to help others? This is challenging stuff! But it's not difficult, or at least it shouldn't be. It was their reflex in the early church and it should be ours today. If we find it hard to give of ourselves and our resources, it's most likely because we've forgotten the life-changing message of the resurrection. New life means new lifestyle.

New power

The strength to do all this does not come from ourselves. We are called by God to live changed lives, and that same God equips us through the Holy Spirit. Nor is it some arbitrary form of help that is given to us: the Spirit is the resurrection Spirit. We pick up the thread in Romans chapter 8.

> You, however, are controlled not by the sinful nature but by the Spirit, if the Spirit of God lives in you. And if anyone does not have the Spirit of Christ, he does not belong to Christ. But if Christ is in you, your body is dead because of sin, yet your spirit is alive because of righteousness. And if the Spirit of him who raised Jesus from the dead is living in you, he who raised Christ from the dead will also give life to your mortal bodies through his Spirit, who lives in you.
> (Romans 8:9–11)

But let's get a couple of things straight first.

A NEW PRESENCE

Notice that Paul says that to have the Spirit is to be Christian, and to be Christian is to have the Spirit. There is no such thing as a Spirit-less Christian, nor could Paul imagine there being a Spirit-indwelt non-Christian. All who are Christian – raised with Christ – are indwelt by the Spirit of God. Notice too the progression in Paul's language: the 'Spirit of God lives in you . . . the Spirit of Christ . . . Christ is in you'. The Spirit of God is the means by which Christ dwells in us. We are 'in' him; he is 'in' us. And if the risen Christ is in us, things are going to look different round here.

This is why, shortly before he died, Jesus said to his disciples that it was better for them that he leave them: 'It is for your good that I am going away' (John 16:7a). It must have been very puzzling for them at the time. How could it possibly be better to not have Jesus around? In our own way, and even from the distance of two millennia later, we can empathize with their confusion. It's easy for us to long to have been there at the time of Jesus. If only we could have seen him or physically heard him. To have been in his presence during that time – surely discipleship would have been so much easier. And yet the same challenge reaches our ears: 'It is for your good that I am going away' (John 16:7a). It is better to be alive in our time, physically absent from Jesus, than to have lived then in his presence. Why? Because in his physical absence Jesus can be spiritually present with us in a far deeper way. 'Unless I go away, the Counsellor will not come to you; but if I go, I will send him to you' (John 16:7b). (By the way 'Counsellor' is one of the names Jesus has for the Holy Spirit, meaning something like 'comforter' or 'strengthener'.) Jesus' logic is clear: his going means the Spirit's coming, and as we've just seen, the Spirit's coming means Christ in us. We are not alone.

And we are certainly not alone as we seek to live transformed lives. Resurrection lifestyle will need the presence of a resurrection Spirit. And that is exactly what we have as Christians. Back to Romans 8: 'The Spirit of him who raised Jesus from the dead is living in you' (Romans 8:11). It must take no less than this to change us, the power God used in raising Christ from the grave. Even with the will to change, in our own strength we cannot take off the old self and live to please God, yet by the Spirit we can at last fight the sin within us.

A LESSON FROM SCHOOL

It might be worth a quick trip to a passage a little earlier in Romans. The presence of Christ in us is further evidence of something Paul has already said:

> If we have been united with him like this in his death, we will certainly also be united with him in his resurrection. For we know that our old self was crucified with him so that the body of sin might be done away with, that we should no longer be slaves to sin – because anyone who has died has been freed from sin.
>
> Now if we died with Christ, we believe that we will also live with him. For we know that since Christ was raised from the dead, he cannot die again; death no longer has mastery over him. The death he died, he died to sin once for all; but the life he lives, he lives to God.
>
> In the same way, count yourselves dead to sin but alive to God in Christ Jesus. Therefore do not let sin reign in your mortal body so that you obey its evil desires. Do not offer the parts of your body to sin, as instruments of wickedness, but rather offer yourselves to God, as those who have been brought from death to life; and offer the parts of your body

to him as instruments of righteousness. For sin shall not be
your master, because you are not under law, but under grace.
(Romans 6:5–14)

Our allegiance to Christ unites us with him, and means that
we are in effect under new ownership. Whereas we had been
'under sin', under its rule and authority, now we belong to
Christ. We have changed masters, changed owners. Paul wants
us to understand this and see what this means. As those united
with Christ in his death and resurrection we have 'been freed
from sin' (verse 7) and sin is no longer our master (verse 14).
It once had authority over us; it no longer does. Because of
that, we need to think about it differently, to regard ourselves
as 'dead to sin but alive to God' (verse 11).

It was about five years after having left school that I returned
for the first time. As a prestigious former pupil (or as someone
who they knew had nothing better to do) I'd been invited to
speak at the main school assembly one morning. It felt very
strange to return, but I walked through the gate with a bit of
a swagger. After all, I'd been through this place and survived.
Unlike all the kids shuffling along beside me (and don't they
all look so *small*) I'd seen a bit of life. I was at the ripe age of
twenty-two after all.

Yet it wasn't long before I felt about fourteen again. Sitting
in the assembly hall it all came flooding back: the musty smell,
the noise of 700 creaky wooden chairs, the same headmaster
giving the same announcements. But then at one point he
suddenly barked out, 'SIT UP STRAIGHT!!' My reflex was to
immediately fix my posture and look like I was paying careful
attention. But he wasn't talking to me. And a thought occurred:
he's not *my* headmaster any more. I don't have to do what he
says. I can *slouch* if I want to. (I didn't, of course.) I had been
so used, over so many years, to doing what that voice told me

to. It had had authority over me, and so it required a conscious effort on my part to not feel bound to it.

Hence Paul says, 'count yourselves dead to sin' (Romans 6:11). It has to do with our minds and how we think. Sin doesn't have authority over us any more, but it will *feel* as though it does. We've obeyed its voice so often in the past and so our reflex is to do what it says. And so we need to *think* differently. We're not under sin any more. We're under new ownership, united to Christ and indwelt by his resurrection Spirit. We don't *have* to sin. It no longer has authority. More than that, as well as being freed from its power, we have a new power with which to resist it and to live as new people.

So, Paul says, by the Spirit we are to 'put to death the misdeeds of the body' (Romans 8:13). The resurrection Spirit is the one by whom we fight sin. And, whether we like it or not, fight we must.

FIGHT . . .

Some people seem to like conflict. They'll cross a street to pick a fight and enjoy nothing more than a good tussle, whether it's physical or verbal. Most of us can't bear conflict and will avoid it whenever we can. But all of us need to face up to it. Being raised with Christ means there's a war on. We need to fight. In fact, according to Paul's language, we need to *kill*. God doesn't want the enemy to be weakened or pacified, but destroyed. And the enemy in this instance is our sinful nature: every instinct from our old self that would have us live for ourselves rather than for God. We are to repudiate all forms of evil in our lives, every use of our body and mind that serves us and not God.

It's only by the Spirit that we can do this, for it takes nothing less than the power which raised Christ from the dead to fight the sin within us. Interestingly, in connection with this battle,

Paul speaks of us being 'led by the Spirit' (Romans 8:14). However else that term might be used by Christians today, it is clear to Paul that the Spirit-led life is one which is battling by the Spirit's power for holiness. A similar connection is made in Paul's letter to the Galatians, where to 'live by the Spirit' is not to 'gratify the desires of the sinful nature' (Galatians 5:16). To 'keep in step with the Spirit' is not to follow some mystical leading but to live as those who have 'crucified the sinful nature with its passions and desires' (Galatians 5:24–25), and show in increasing measure the Christ-like fruit of that Spirit. In other words, to live a resurrection life.

'Put to death' and 'crucify' are hardly attractive phrases, and no less so in Paul's time. Crucifixion remains one of the most torturous forms of death yet devised. Paul's language is emotive, and intentionally so. In the heat of temptation we need to remember this vivid imagery if we are to persevere in our quest for holiness. We will not drift into it. It won't come through passivity. We need to take up arms and fight, and by the resurrection Spirit we can – in him we have new power.

. . . AND THINK

This all means that we need to fight our sin with the carrot, not the stick. It is easy to look through this teaching and to think, 'Right. I have *got* to try harder on all this.' It's not entirely wrong as a response, but it's hardly right either. The point of it all, once again, is grace. Grace has saved us and raised us up. By grace God has now come to live in us. His presence lends us strength and power to live for him. Holy living cannot be even remotely experienced unless we remember this grace and all that God has done for us.

When I am next conscious of temptation, I need to remember all this, to walk myself through it: God is in me to change me and help me to live differently. He gives me the grace to fight sin, and even when I fail I can come back to the grace that has forgiven me and fully accepts me.

In the moment of temptation, sin feels good – it feels warm and right. When it is a sin that has done business with us in the past, it also feels inevitable, like an old friend we can't say 'no' to. It is at this point I need to remember the resurrection. This particular sin is not inevitable any more. I am not bound to it any longer. I am free not to fall into it. Bad habits of even many years *can* be changed. I need to count myself dead to sin.

New ambition

Being raised with Christ means we have a fight in the present, but it also means we yearn for something in the future. Alongside mortification (putting to death what is evil) comes aspiration (longing for what it good). Both flow from the resurrection.

In Philippians 3 Paul celebrates the surpassing greatness of knowing Christ. It has changed everything, not least his former estimation of himself. Paul's confidence is no longer in his religious prowess, his background or achievements (though there was evidently a lot to impress). Things he would once have boasted in are now nothing to him: 'rubbish', akin to something you'd throw in the dustbin or flush down the toilet. Evidence of this change of thinking is the new ambition that flows from it. From his Christian vantage point Paul now knows exactly what he wants: 'I want to know Christ and the power of his resurrection' (Philippians 3:10).

AMBITION 1: TO KNOW CHRIST

This is amazing. By this time Paul has followed Jesus for about thirty years. He's written letters like Romans and Galatians. He's written theology that will have Christians excited, daunted, confused and worshipping for centuries to come. He's not a new convert. He's not a rookie. He's well into his spiritual middle age, and yet we don't see any middle-age spread. Just an undiminished hunger to know Christ.

We say, 'Paul, *you* know him. Believe me, you know him! Slow down a bit – you're doing fine. We're still trying to keep up with you. Give us a sec to catch our breath!'

Paul says, 'Yes, but I want to *know* him. There's so much more and I still feel like I've only just begun.'

My favourite scene in C. S. Lewis's *Chronicles of Narnia* comes in *Prince Caspian*. It has been a long time since Lucy and her friends have seen Aslan, and Lucy is the first to encounter him again. At first she is surprised.

> 'Aslan,' said Lucy, 'you're bigger.'
> 'That is because you are older, little one,' answered he.
> 'Not because you are?'
> 'I am not. But every year you grow you will find me bigger.'[2]

The more Paul knows Christ, the more there is to know. Jesus just keeps on getting bigger.

AMBITION 2: TO KNOW CHRIST'S OBEDIENCE

Bound up with knowing Christ is knowing the power of his resurrection. Not a mega-wattage experience to thrill him, but *resurrection* power: life-giving and life-changing. This is not the power of worldly strength and brilliance, nor of ministerial triumph, but power that will lead to Christ-likeness. It's not an easy power to manifest, for it involves sharing in Jesus' sufferings. As we've seen, it involves a battle. The path Christ trod was hard and painful. He was known as the 'man of sorrows' (Isaiah 53:3). And yet Paul strives to follow in his steps, to be 'like him in his death'. What was Christ like in his death? Paul has already told us: 'He was *obedient* to death – even death on a cross!' (Philippians 2:8, my emphasis). Paul longs for resurrection power to lead him into obedience to God, and in doing so to grow in likeness of Christ.

Paul also knows that to be like Christ in his death is to be like him in his risen life. Back in Romans 8 Paul told us that 'if the Spirit of him who raised Jesus from the dead is living in you, he who raised Christ from the dead will also give life to your mortal bodies through his Spirit, who lives in you' (Romans 8:11). If the Spirit's present work in us involves empowering us to live lives of holiness, his future work is to raise us as he raised Christ. He is committed to us for the long haul.

So now Paul can speak of his confidence of that future resurrection, ' . . . becoming like him in his death, and so, somehow, to attain to the resurrection from the dead' (Philippians 3:10b–11). The 'somehow' is not an indication of doubt about whether this will happen, but an admission of agnosticism on his part as to precisely *how* this will happen. Maybe Christ will return, or maybe Paul will die and 'be with Christ' (1:23). He does not know in a blow-by-blow account what will be involved in either scenario. But he does know it will happen: he will attain to the resurrection of the dead.

FOLLOWING PAUL'S EXAMPLE

Paul's ambition is shaped by the resurrection. In fact, it's shaped by two resurrections, and Paul is aware that he lives between them: the resurrection of Christ on the third day, and the resurrection of the dead on the last day. He longs for the power of that first resurrection to produce in him increasing Christ-likeness, and he fixes his eyes on the end when he will experience in his physical body the transformation of that final resurrection. He calls on us to follow him in his ambition, to follow his example and to see ahead of us what he sees ahead of him: 'Join with others in following my example' (Philippians 3:17).

The first mountain I ever hiked was a dormant volcano in Kenya's Rift Valley. The heat and altitude, combined with my general lack of fitness, made it very hard work. The slope was steep, dry and dusty. I tried to match the steps of the friend just ahead of me on the trail, and to delay rewarding myself with a backward look at the deepening view behind me until I'd gained enough height to feel that I'd earned it.

Someone on another hike once quoted the line of a poem he'd studied as a kid about mountain walking: 'every level step a holiday'.[3] Halfway up a mountain in the middle of the scorched Rift Valley, any step that didn't involve pulling myself upwards would have been a holiday indeed. Needless to say, my brain was switched to Melodrama Mode, producing regular reports about my never being able to get to the top: *too tired . . . too hot . . . too far . . . too unfit.*

One moment changed all that. A friend who had been further ahead suddenly called down to me. He was still an implausible distance away but had just reached the rim of the crater. 'Sam!' he shouted down. 'You are going to *love* this!' It wasn't his words but the expression on his face that did it for me. He was looking down at the volcano crater spread out before him, a sight celebrated for its breathtaking beauty. He looked stunned and amazed. Right then I wanted to be seeing what he was seeing. I was suddenly awash with adrenaline, and pushed my way up to his position in a matter of minutes. I was rewarded with the most spectacular view I've ever seen in my life.

Paul has his eyes on something. What he knows to be ahead of him has filled his horizon and so he strains towards it with every ounce of strength he can muster. He wants us to follow.

We see where his gaze is fixed – on the resurrection of the dead – and we too are filled with new ambition. We can begin to see what he is seeing. And so we push on!

Change I can believe in

We finish where we began: 'Do not offer the parts of your body to sin, as instruments of wickedness, but rather offer yourselves to God, as those who have been brought from death to life' (Romans 6:13).

We want to change. We know God wants us to change. We need to see that holiness is a function of resurrection life. We have been brought from death to life – raised with Christ. On that basis and through that power we are to offer ourselves to God. Resurrection living is holy living.

A few years ago a man in the United States decided to have the Nike Swoosh tattooed onto his chest. When asked why, he replied that he wanted to be able to look down at it in the shower to remind him at the start of each day to 'Just do it'.

Christ has been raised from the dead. In him we are raised to new life. This spiritual resurrection gives us the power and the motivation to lead changed lives. Being raised in Christ means we must not tolerate too low a standard of holiness in our own life, as if it were somehow acceptable to reduce our expectations and goals for godliness. No. We've been raised with Christ, and as those who have been brought from death to life we must now offer ourselves to God.

3

Hope

'Hope' for dummies . . .

I was hoping – hoping quite hard, as it happens. The first two-thirds of the flight had gone smoothly. I'd befriended the old lady in the seat next to me and was munching my way through her bag of candy. But it all came to an abrupt halt when the aircraft made a sudden lurch to the left, as if the pilot was making a handbrake turn. Severe turbulence followed, and lasted till virtually the end of the flight. It felt as though the plane was advancing solely by means of some unseen force repeatedly drop-kicking it across the Atlantic skies. And so I sat there, hands gripping each armrest, hoping – *really* hoping – that the plane would just hurry up and get down onto the ground. Preferably all of it at the same time.

I think we often get hope wrong. We normally speak of hope as something we do: I hope it doesn't rain tomorrow, hope the meeting goes well, and hope this cold clears up. Hopes in these cases can be significant or insignificant – anything from how someone might respond to a marriage proposal to the weekend sports results. But they're pretty much always uncertain. We don't control the things we hope for. I have no power over weather, health, aviation or what side of bed my football team decide to get out of. This kind of hope is another way of describing wishful thinking. It's about things we want, but might not necessarily get. It's fraught with the risk of disappointment and so we 'try not to get our hopes up'. There's every chance it's not going to turn out the way we hoped.

The Bible speaks of hope as something we have. It is about looking forward to something that is certain. I have the hope of eternity with Christ. We still don't control the thing for which we have hope, but God does and has promised eternity to us. There is no degree of risk or disappointment. This hope cannot be frustrated by anyone. Unlike all our other expressions of hope, this is hope that won't disappoint us (as Paul says in Romans 5:5). It is guaranteed by God himself and bears his signature: the resurrection of Jesus from the dead.

This sort of hope makes living possible, for it gives us a future. Part of what makes us human is the ability to consider the future. We can't help but be conscious of it. And we need to be. We need to have a future which is, to some extent, sorted out. We need to have hope.

Hope and humanness

To be without hope is one of the hardest experiences in life. A moment's reflection bears this out. It has been said by those who survived the horrors of the Soviet labour camps in the mid-twentieth century that there were really only two kinds of people imprisoned there: those who had hope, and those who did not. It was the difference between those who could keep going, and those who couldn't. If you take away a person's hope, you take away his or her life. We need to know we have a future to head towards.

This can often be difficult for those heading into middle age. By this stage of life it can become painfully clear what we are actually going to be able to achieve. Realism kicks in. We dream in youth but wake in midlife. A middle-aged man recently said to me, 'By your forties life is pretty much where it's going to be.' The midlife crunch is epitomized by Billy Crystal's character Mitch in the classic 1990s movie *City Slickers*. Mitch sums up the despair of a forty-something by asking his boss one day, 'Have you ever had that feeling that this is the best I'm ever gonna do, this is the best I'm ever gonna feel . . . and it ain't that great?' (His boss, familiar with where all this has come from, sighs in response, 'Happy Birthday, Mitch'.)

By mid-life our options are more limited. It becomes clear that many of our cherished dreams may not materialize in the way we'd always imagined – dreams about family, security, advancement, money, popularity. Where we've got to by this stage pretty much indicates where we'll ever get to. 'Where we're at, is where we're at. And that's it', as I heard one forty-something put it. No wonder they say middle age is the hardest stage of life. It is when hope is doused in the cold water of reality.

A new kind of hope

Christians, by definition, are people of hope. Hope that has the fingerprints and guarantee of God all over it. It all has to do with the resurrection: 'Praise be to the God and Father of our Lord Jesus Christ! In his great mercy he has given us new birth into a living hope through the resurrection of Jesus Christ from the dead' (1 Peter 1:3).

We can see why this hope is so different. It is not based on my circumstances and prospects. It comes through Jesus' resurrection, and is therefore independent of those things. For this reason, it is a *living* hope. It has a life of its own that can endure even the worst experiences of life in this world. It is grounded in what God has done in raising Jesus from the dead. It is hope that is totally contingent on a particular event. And because that event *has happened* our hope is secure. Not wishful-thinking hope, but guaranteed hope.

We need to see how this is so, how Peter is able to connect the resurrection of Jesus two millennia ago with a future hope for Christians today. It's a connection we need to get right, and yet the early Christians got it terribly wrong in two ways, and we need to learn from their mistakes.

Mistake 1: 'The resurrection has already taken place'

This, we're told, is the teaching of Hymenaeus and Philetus, two names that wreak havoc not just on the spellchecker but on the Christian faith as well. Paul discusses them – and others like them – in 2 Timothy:

> Their teaching will spread like gangrene. Among them are Hymenaeus and Philetus, who have wandered away from the truth. They say that the resurrection has already taken place, and they destroy the faith of some.
> (2 Timothy 2:17–18)

According to their teaching the resurrection has already happened: not just that the resurrection of Jesus has happened (which Paul has affirmed many times), but that the whole resurrection 'package' is now done. In other words, Jesus' resurrection was the end of what God is up to, and not the beginning. There is nothing more to come. This idea destroys faith, for it denies the basis of Christian hope.

Paul describes these two faith-wreckers as having wandered away from the truth. Wandering can seem so innocuous and yet be so deadly. In the case of Hymenaeus and Philetus it may have been gradual and incremental, barely noticed by anybody else. But their route had taken them far from the path of Christian truth. Their teaching may have looked and sounded Christian, but it was not a way of thinking that God would have anything to do with. They had redefined resurrection hope and changed its tense, relegating it to the past, and in the process devastating Christian faith.

We're not given the particulars about how they did this, but there are two ways in which it can be done. And both are with us still today, luring us to one side before mugging us of true gospel hope. Let's consider each.

'WE HAVE IT ALL NOW'

First, some will say that all that we hope for in the resurrection is available now. All the fullness for which we long can actually be enjoyed in the present. There's nothing left to wait for, just a bit of mopping up at the end. The best can be experienced now. So, such teachers say, we don't need to wait for full victory over sin. We don't need to wait to be free of ill-health. Heaven can be had today. But you must have enough faith. Believe it and you'll receive it.

This thinking wanders from the truth. It misunderstands what we receive and when. As we will see, it ignores the blessings that are ours in Christ, but for which we must wait. Yes, there is much we enjoy now as Christians: the reality of forgiveness, the presence and work of God's Spirit, the new matrix of relationships that results from being fellow-members of God's family with other believers. But we still must wait for the end before we enjoy the fullness of what we have in Christ. To claim we have it all now raises expectations and ruins faith. It can't possibly deliver and so it implies that God is not all he's cracked up to be. It leads to spiritual breakdowns and breeds cynicism.

'THIS IS ALL THERE IS'

Second, others will say that the resurrection spoken of in the New Testament is a metaphor. It is not a supernatural miracle, but a picture of what this world can become. Heaven and hell are not external spiritual realities, but are just the very best and the very worst of life in *this* world. What we know today is all there is. We are not waiting for any future miraculous intervention in this world by God. The resurrection is another way of looking at this world as it currently is, not evidence of some different future reality.

Again, this thinking ignores scriptural truth and Christian experience. It is clear that the Gospel writers did not regard the resurrection of Jesus as a kind of parable. The resurrection narratives don't read as fiction, but as historical fact. We are given specifics: people, places, times and names. It happened and we can check it out. There are those today, sometimes within the church, who insist on treating miracles as metaphors. Jesus feeding 5,000 people with a tiny amount of food, they tell us, is just a metaphor for the importance of sharing. None of it is meant to be taken in any literal sense.

Those who treat the miracles in the Bible this way often do so because they cannot accept the concept of supernatural work in this world. Their teaching reflects a view of this world that excludes any kind of miraculous intervention, and so they are forced to come up with alternative explanations when such interventions do happen. On the surface such people may seem Christian, for they speak of God, Jesus and the Spirit, after all, but deep down they are materialists: material reality – what we can see and touch – is the only reality. They believe in God, but limit his activity to the natural processes of this world. It is the worst of both worlds: materialism without the lie-in on a Sunday morning; religion without the power. But the bodily resurrection of Jesus overturns this thinking. It is not that faithful Christians can't do proper history, but that these materialists can't do proper theology.

Mistake 2: 'There is no resurrection of the dead'

This second kind of false teaching about the resurrection stems from a different issue. We found the first in Ephesus; this kind Paul discovered rife in Corinth: 'But if it is preached that Christ has been raised from the dead, how can some of you say that there is no resurrection of the dead?' (1 Corinthians 15:12).

The issue seems quite specific: it was being taught in Corinth that there was no physical resurrection to come. This teaching reflected the prevailing belief in Corinth that the spiritual was what ultimately mattered; the physical was merely a corrupt and unpleasant casing for the real, spiritual stuff within us. By this reckoning our physical bodies didn't matter much, and so you found some Christians in Corinth sleeping with prostitutes (1 Corinthians 6:15–16), and others, even though they were married, abstaining from sex altogether (1 Corinthians 7:4–5). In both cases it stemmed from a low view of the body.

Paul had already done much to correct this view. In response to the sexual sins of some of the Corinthian Christians, Paul reminded them that their bodies were not a matter of spiritual indifference. They had been bought at great cost (1 Corinthians 6:20). They now belonged to Jesus (see 1 Corinthians 6:19). How they used their bodies was therefore a reflection of their view of Jesus. We are to honour Jesus with our bodies. We must have a lower view of sexual sin and a higher view of marital sex. And because our bodies belong to him in the present, Jesus has plans for them. Our bodies have a future. They will be physically raised and transformed.

The resurrection confirms the goodness of what God has made. We have a physical hope and, as we'll see in due course, so does creation.

Resurrection hope for the Christian

Paul is at pains to show the Corinthian church the importance of the physical resurrection to come. Quite simply, if there is no bodily resurrection (in the future) then Jesus was not himself bodily raised from the dead (in the past): 'If there is no resurrection from the dead, then not even Christ has been raised' (1 Corinthians 15:13). This is serious.

Playing Jenga with belief

It's worth bearing in mind that Christian truth – Christian theology – is integrated. It is all of a piece and hangs together in such a way that if we fiddle about with one part all the rest is affected. We cannot alter one part of biblical truth and expect all the other parts to stay the same. Truth is interconnected. If you decide there is no physical resurrection from the dead (that is, that there is no physical future for us after we die), you deny the resurrection of Christ. Do that and, like carelessly whipping out a foundation block in the game Jenga, the whole thing starts to collapse around you, as Paul is about to show. Muck about with the resurrection of Jesus, and you'll discover you don't have much of a gospel left.

So, says Paul to the Corinthians, let's run for a while with your theory. No physical resurrection means no physical resurrection of Jesus. And what would that mean? Well, everything, as it turns out. The nature of our hope for the future is bound up with the nature of Jesus' resurrection in the past. We are only able to look forward to our resurrection if we can first look back at his. The significance of Jesus' bodily resurrection shows us the nature of our bodily resurrection.

The importance of Jesus' bodily resurrection

What if the resurrection of Jesus had never happened? Paul is about to show us.

If Jesus has not been raised

They call it 'counterfactual history'. It is that part of historiography that deals with the 'what if?' questions. What if the 1066 invasion had been repelled? What if George Washington's army had lost the Revolutionary War? Sometimes the factors involved are so complex that it becomes little more than speculation. But the value of counterfactual history is that it highlights the importance of particular details. At times, history is determined by seemingly insignificant developments. Change those and you discover that seconds can affect centuries.

One example comes from the 2009 Tom Cruise movie *Valkyrie*. His character, von Stauffenberg, is a high-ranking German army officer involved in an attempt to assassinate Adolf Hitler in 1943. The key moment comes at a briefing at which both men are present. Von Stauffenberg's briefcase contains explosives, and he carefully leaves it under the table and exits the room. Had the briefcase remained untouched, the blast would certainly have killed Hitler, the plot would have succeeded, and history would have been significantly different. So what went wrong? The briefcase bumped against the foot of one of the colonels sitting there, who moved it round the other side of a heavy table leg. This then absorbed a significant amount of the blast, saving Hitler's life.

In order to make his point, Paul engages in a bit of his own counterfactual history. What if Jesus did not rise from the dead? Where would that leave us? Paul doesn't need to speculate – it's as clear as day: 'If Christ has not been raised, our preaching is useless and so is your faith' (1 Corinthians 15:14).

Two things are affected, and both are incredibly significant: Paul's preaching and our faith.

PAUL'S PREACHING

If Jesus did not rise then Paul and his colleagues were *wrong*, plain and simple: 'We are then found to be false witnesses about God, for we have testified about God that he raised Christ from the dead' (1 Corinthians 15:15). It means the apostles have got God wrong. And therefore they have got his gospel wrong. Their preaching is useless if their belief is incorrect. A witness whose testimony is false is not one whose words warrant any consideration.

We need to remember that Christianity has something of a special relationship with history. What we believe is bound up with particular events of history in a way that many other religions and belief systems are often not. Take Buddhism, for example. If you were to be able to prove historically that Gautama, Buddhism's founder, never existed, then nothing would change. It would not change or undermine the beliefs of Buddhists. Buddhism is not historically contingent. Its core beliefs are non-historical.

Not so Christianity. The Christian gospel is grounded in history. It has to do with particular historical events: chiefly, the life, death and resurrection of Jesus. If someone could prove that Jesus never existed, or that he wasn't crucified, or that he never rose again, then Christianity would be completely undermined. Paul's message would be useless. Good for nothing. That same message on our lips, shared with friends, colleagues, relatives and neighbours, would be nothing but hot air and wasted effort. It would be empty of any power, for it would not be God's truth. How futile Paul's life and ministry would turn out to be: all that hardship and opposition, all the heartache and deprivation – all of it for nothing if Jesus had not risen.

But don't sit there feeling sorry for Paul. If Jesus Christ is still dead you have some serious problems of your own.

OUR FAITH

And if Christ has not been raised, your faith is futile; you are still in your sins. Then also those who have fallen asleep [that is, those who have died] in Christ are lost. If only for this life we have hope in Christ, we are to be pitied more than all men. (1 Corinthians 15:17–19)

People today often say that it's important to be a person of faith, to have some kind of spiritual belief. Something to lean on – doesn't really matter what it is, exactly, just that you have it. Paul disagrees. There is such a thing as *futile* faith, a faith that is absolutely worthless. The question to ask is not 'Do I have faith?' But 'What is my faith in?' What matters is not the presence of faith, but the object of that faith. Sincerity is not enough, for you can be sincerely wrong. Sincere faith in something hopeless is not going to get you anywhere.

THE 'ALLBERRY THEOREM'

Let me provide an example. I have an older brother. Younger siblings know that this is a decidedly mixed blessing. An older brother is a competitor: a bigger rival for the limited amount of food, toys and parental affection to be found in the house. But an older brother can also be useful. Mine went to the same school as me. This meant that I could say I knew some of the older boys in school, which afforded a certain amount of protection. It also meant that my brother had sat through the same third-year physics exam two years previously. This was key. My aptitude for physics never extended beyond the discovery that if you stir Marmite with a fork for long enough it eventually turns white. I needed all the help I could get.

So you'll appreciate how good it was to discover, in the run-up to this exam, that the questions hadn't changed for years and that my brother could remember some of them exactly – and, more to the point, the answers too. One such question concerned a plane carrying a load. Imagine that plane is flying overhead in the same direction as you are now facing and that, at the precise moment it's directly above you, it decides to drop its cargo. Would the cargo land (a) somewhere in front of you, (b) on you, or (c) somewhere behind you? Bear in mind that the plane is, say, 30,000 feet above you and travelling at 500 miles per hour. Think about it. Most people answer (a), given the enormous forward momentum of the plane at the time it drops the load. Most people are right. But my brother remembered the answer as being (c), and so that was the answer I dutifully gave.

The first warning sign should have been when the teacher overseeing the exam happened to walk past my desk as I gave this answer, paused, looked down at my paper and pointing to the question, whispered, 'Are you *sure*?' And he was a PE teacher. When a PE teacher needs to correct your physics you know something has gone wrong. But I stuck to my guns. After the exam, we all shared how we'd found it and I discovered I was the only one to have put (c). I still stuck to my guns. My brother had told me, I said proudly. I was sincere. And I was wrong. For a number of years it was referred to as the 'Allberry Theorem of Physics'.

It is possible to have a faith that is worthless. If Christ has not been raised, that is the exact kind of faith we Christians have. And we should be pitied above all others. It changes everything. If Christ is still dead and buried then there is no point to being Christian. Sincerity makes no difference. We may sincerely feel the acceptance of God, but if Jesus is not alive we are still in our sins. He claimed his death would be our ransom. But if his death was the end we have no reason to think his crucifixion achieved anything. There has been no victory over sin and its corollary. Death still reigns.

We cannot remove the bodily resurrection of Jesus and think the house of cards is going to remain standing. No resurrection means Paul's preaching is useless, and our faith is futile.

So this is what it means if Jesus has not been raised from the dead. We lose everything. But what is the flip side? What follows given that Jesus *has* been raised? A lot, says Paul.

If Jesus has been raised

> But Christ has indeed been raised from the dead, the firstfruits of those who have fallen asleep. For since death came through a man, the resurrection of the dead comes also through a man. For as in Adam all die, so in Christ all will be made alive. But each in his own turn: Christ, the firstfruits; then, when he comes, those who belong to him.
>
> (1 Corinthians 15:20–23)

JESUS THE FIRST OF MANY

There is a lot in these verses to untangle, but Paul's point is clear: the resurrection of Jesus was not a one-off event. His was to be the first of many. Paul twice describes the raising of Jesus as the 'firstfruits' – that initial part of the harvest that indicates more is to come. All who are in Christ will be made alive; his resurrection shows what will happen to all the rest. The resurrection of Jesus is the guarantee and demonstration of what is to come for those who trust in him.

Someone once said it was like watching slow-motion footage of a dam bursting. At first there is only a slight bulge in the dam wall as the water presses against a weakness in the structure. Then a crack appears, followed quickly by a small spurt of water. The spurt becomes a jet and before long the entire section of dam wall gives way and the whole lake empties through it. It started with just one small spurt. But in a way that small spurt guaranteed that the rest was to come. Where it went, the rest was sure to follow. The same is true of Christ and those united to him: where he goes we will follow. In his resurrection he is the first of many.

JESUS THE KING OF ALL

Then the end will come, when he hands over the kingdom to God the Father after he has destroyed all dominion, authority and power. For he must reign until he has put all his enemies under his feet. The last enemy to be destroyed is death. For he 'has put everything under his feet'. Now when it says that 'everything' has been put under him, it is clear that this does not include God himself, who put everything under Christ. When he has done this, then the Son himself will be made subject to him who put everything under him, so that God may be all in all.
(1 Corinthians 15:24–28)

Jesus is also the King of all. His resurrection typifies what will happen to those who follow him, but in another sense it is quite unique. As we have already seen, the resurrection of Jesus demonstrates his lordship. It is the sign that his enemies are at last being put under his feet. Death has been dealt the fatal blow and will one day be destroyed. He is the Son to whom is given rule over the whole of creation. As Paul has already told us, he 'was declared with power to be the Son of God, by his resurrection from the dead: Jesus Christ our Lord' (Romans 1:4). This is the gospel. The crucified Saviour is now the risen Lord.

It is clear, then, that the basis of our hope as Christians is the resurrection of Jesus. As we look back at the basis of our hope, we are then able to look forward to what is the content of our hope: bodily resurrection in the future.

The nature of our bodily resurrection

What has happened in the past shows us what will happen in the future. Like Jesus, we are to be raised physically from the dead. Through faith, as we have seen, we are united to him. His Spirit dwells within us: 'And if the Spirit of him who raised Jesus from the dead is living in you, he who raised Christ from the dead *will also give life to your mortal bodies* through his Spirit, who lives in you' (Romans 8:11, my emphasis). The Spirit within us is the Spirit of resurrection. What that Spirit did in raising Jesus he will do for us. We are guaranteed bodily resurrection.

Resurrection questions

But we do not need to dwell on this for long before a whole host of questions comes flooding to mind. Back to 1 Corinthians 15, where Paul has some of these questions in mind: 'How are the dead raised? With what kind of body will they come?' (1 Corinthians 15:35).

Try to imagine your future resurrection for a moment and you will begin asking these questions. How will it all work? What age will I be when I'm resurrected – a baby? – a teen? Will I have to go through acne and a squeaky voice all over again? Or will I be old? And what will my body be like? Will I be athletic? Will a broken nose still be broken? Will I have blue eyes this time round?

There are all sorts of details we want to know about. Those questions were just a taster. I don't have a clue how it is all going to work. But given I'm not the one who has to decide how it's all going to work, I don't need to worry. In fact, it is plain stupid to worry about it (1 Corinthians 15:36). There is a difference between not knowing everything, and not knowing anything. And what we *can* know is more than enough to stop us worrying about what we *can't* know. So, what will our bodily resurrection be like? Paul says we should look at nature, and then look at the risen Christ.

Look at nature

Paul is gloved-up, wearing green boots and heading for the garden. We need to learn some things from nature – three things as it turns out.

LESSON 1: PUT DEATH IN, GET LIFE OUT . . .

First, there needs to be death in order to be life. 'What you sow does not come to life unless it dies' (1 Corinthians 15:36). The seed 'dies' when we sow it. You shove it into the ground and leave it there, buried. It is, to all intents and purposes, dead. Yet from this death comes life, and without this death there would not be life. Leave the seed in the packet or on the table and not much is going to happen. It has to 'die' first. Death is a condition of resurrection. It's true of seeds and it's true of us. Our bodies need to die in order to be raised up in new physical life. The transformation God wants to bring to us physically can't happen unless our present body dies.

LESSON 2: WHAT YOU GET OUT WASN'T WHAT YOU PUT IN . . .

New life comes from death, but the second lesson is that the new life which emerges is different from what was sown. 'When you sow, you do not plant the body that will be, but just a seed, perhaps of wheat or of something else (1 Corinthians 15:37). Paul is a little unrealistic about the level of interest I have in gardening, but all the same I made a trip to the local garden centre to buy some seed and investigate for myself.

I have before me some seed for sweet corn, carrots and cauliflower (sorry, Paul, they were out of wheat). There is little correspondence between what it looks like as a seed and when fully grown. The carrot seed (much to my disappointment) is not orange and carrot-shaped – a smaller version of the final product. Without the packet to tell me, I would have no idea what kind of seeds they were. I certainly couldn't have guessed just from their appearance. But 'God gives it a body as he has determined' (1 Corinthians 15:38).

It is Agriculture 101: what you shove into the ground is different from what you dig up out of it several months later. Our new, resurrected body will be different from the old. It's not such an absurd idea – it is all around us in nature.

LESSON 3: 'LIKE, DUH . . . '

The third lesson Paul has for us from nature is more broad: 'All flesh is not the same: Men have one kind of flesh, animals have another, birds another and fish another' (1 Corinthians 15:39). It feels a little patronizing to be told this – I can tell the difference between a goldfish and an elephant, thanks – but that is precisely Paul's point: God is pretty experienced when it comes to finding appropriate bodies for things. We may be floored by some of the questions that come to us about the resurrection of the dead, but do you really think that God, who has made the countless kinds of creature on this earth, is going to struggle to make an appropriate body for those who are raised in Christ?

Look down at the creatures and look up at the heavens (1 Corinthians 15:40–41). There is seemingly an infinite number of bodies in this universe. There are more than 13,000 species of fern and 12,000 species of moss. This is something of an area of expertise for God. Do you really think he will have trouble providing a resurrection body for you? The huge variety in creation shows we have no worries here. God is not limited to what we can imagine or understand. His creative power is boundless.

Look at the risen Christ

We can look beyond nature. The next step in understanding the nature of our bodily resurrection is to look at the nature of Christ's resurrected body. Just as there was correspondence between us and Adam, the first man, Paul shows there will also be correspondence between us and the risen Jesus, the new Adam. Both are prototypes of those to follow. 'Just as we have borne the likeness of the earthly man, so shall we bear the likeness of the man from heaven' (1 Corinthians 15:49). Jesus' resurrection body tells us about ours. He will transform our lowly bodies, Paul says elsewhere, 'so that they will be like his glorious body' (Philippians 3:21).

What was the resurrection body of Jesus like? The Gospel accounts show us that there was continuity and discontinuity with his pre-resurrection body.

CHRIST'S RISEN BODY

Let's consider the continuity: Jesus bore the scars of his crucifixion (John 20:25, 27). He was still recognizably the man his disciples had known (Luke 24:39). He ate with them (Luke 24:42–43) and broke bread with them (Luke 24:30–31).

But there were also differences. He was recognizable, but not immediately so (John 21:4). Two of his disciples shared a long journey with him, all the while unaware that it was actually him they were walking with and talking to (Luke 24:15–16, though Luke adds that they were 'kept from recognising him' indicating that there was more to their lack of recognition than just a change in how Jesus looked). It was far more than his appearance: his nature seemed different from what had gone before. The risen Jesus seemed to pass through locked doors (John 20:26), and suddenly to appear and disappear (John 21:1, Luke 24:31). He was less bound by the physical limitations of normal human life. His body had changed.

This is some indication of what we have to look forward to in our own bodily resurrection. There will be continuity and also discontinuity. I will be recognizably and authentically *me*. But I will be a *transformed* me. And I take it this transformation will be a more authentic me than I am now. I will be more fully myself then than I have ever been.

Our risen bodies

Paul compares our pre- and post-resurrection bodies.

> So will it be with the resurrection of the dead. The body that is sown is perishable, it is raised imperishable; it is sown in dishonour, it is raised in glory; it is sown in weakness, it is raised in power; it is sown a natural body, it is raised a spiritual body.
>
> If there is a natural body, there is also a spiritual body.
> (1 Corinthians 15:42–44)

The contrast relates to four areas:

- **My body now is perishable**. It will one day fall apart and decompose. In our prime we may feel strong and indestructible, but one day people will stand at our graveside. Our bodies will die and decay. They have a limited shelf-life. They are not designed to go on for ever. Modern toasters and kettles apparently have a form of obsolescence built into them. Our fallen bodies certainly do. They function for only a limited time. Death is inevitable. The visible signs of ageing are a picture of this. But this will not be so with our resurrection bodies. They will be imperishable. They will go on for ever.

- **My body now is dishonourable**. It has been a vehicle for sin. To my shame, I have used my feet to take me to places of ungodliness. I have used my eyes to look with lust, my hands to harm others, my tongue to lie or exaggerate or humiliate. I have offered parts of my body to sin, as 'instruments of wickedness' (Romans 6:13). My body has also suffered because of sin: bruised by others, misused and poorly stewarded by myself. Paul has already reminded his Corinthian readers that sexual sin is a sin against our own body (1 Corinthians 6:18): it changes us – something seemingly organic happens in the act of sexual sin that means we are not the same again. Our bodies are dishonourable. But our new bodies will be raised in glory. Rather than bearing the memories and marks of sin, they will shine. They will be like Jesus' 'glorious body'.

- **My body now is weak**. It is easily damaged or slowed down. I have scars on my torso from two major operations. I seem to get a cold around September that never really goes away until May, when I enjoy two weeks of robust health and then get a summer cold. I'm allergic to cat hair. All it takes to reduce me to a puffy-eyed, sniffling wreck is the presence of some kitten fur: that's weakness! I suspect that most of us, even in relative youth, are on medication for something. I asked a congregation of about 300, mostly made up of undergraduate students, to put up a hand if they'd had any kind of medication in the previous seven days. There was a forest of raised hands. Isaiah reminds us that 'even youths grow tired and weary' (Isaiah 40:30). Even in our primes we're not that impressive. It gets worse when we're older. If, one Sunday morning, I ask a group of elderly church members to describe their physical ailments, I'll need to cancel dinner plans. Our bodies are weak. We need to spend a third of our lives sleeping, after all. But our new bodies will be raised in power. They will not be subject to the same limitations and vulnerabilities. Our strength will be renewed and we will 'soar on wings like eagles' (Isaiah 40:31). We will be able to do then what is impossible for us now.

- **My body now is natural**. That is, it belongs to this realm of nature. It is from the dust of this fallen world, and is appropriate for this kind of life. But my future body, though still physical, will be supernatural. It will be the perfect vehicle for glorifying God in the new creation. My future is supernatural. The very best of human resources and technology now could not come close to achieving for my body what will happen when it is raised. It will belong then to a new order, fitted for service in a new, everlasting realm.

This is our hope. Our future is very much physical. Contrary to the view most people have of heaven, our ultimate destiny is physical. We will not be floating around disembodied in the middle of some cloudy vista. We will have *bodies*, risen, transformed glorious bodies.

We can see why Peter described this as a 'living' hope. It is not subject to the terms and conditions attached so often to earthly expectation. It is sure and certain. Nothing will thwart it. It is hope that looks beyond death.

WHEN GREY HAIR IS GOOD!

This is the major difference between Christian hope and any other kind. Our Western society cannot bear to think about death. The only hope it can find is a form that hides away all forms and reminders of death. But true hope is not found in hiding from death, but in being able to come to terms with its reality. For Christians, death is not the end, but a new beginning. It is the condition for resurrection.

For Christians, death is not the end, but a new beginning. It is the condition for resurrection.

One Christian lady in her mid-fifties told me recently that this is why she doesn't bother to dye her hair. She said she doesn't mind the process of ageing affecting her appearance. Her perspective has been shaped by resurrection hope. The best is not behind her; it is to come. The body I have and am – *this* body now – is not ultimate. Even at its peak it doesn't come close to the body I will have. Grey hairs are therefore not a threat but a promise. The gradual slowing down of the body, the processes of physical ageing and decay that anticipate our final passing, these are not (to borrow a phrase) the beginning of the end, but just the end of the beginning. Better is to come – much better! Death is the transition to resurrection. We can therefore look it in the eye: it has lost its sting.

> Where, O death, is your victory?
> Where, O death, is your sting?
> (1 Corinthians 15:55)

Most of us hate or fear wasps and bees precisely because of their sting. But if I knew that, somehow, the sting of these creatures had been removed, would I really go into contortions every time one hovered nearby? A stingless wasp would be one we could swat away playfully. No threat at all.

Well, we now have only a stingless death ahead of us. This is not to trivialize the pain that might come with death, for us and for those we leave behind. But it is to recognize that it has been robbed of its greatest sting: sin. Death is not now the prelude to judgment and condemnation, but to a new, perfected life. Christians can approach it differently. We have hope – living, breathing, growing hope.

The New Testament does not stop there. Our hope is not unphysical, nor is it just individual. There is hope for the Christian, but there is also hope for creation, to which we now turn.

Resurrection hope for creation

Deadly beauty

The first Westerner to discover it described it as the 'most beautiful view in Africa'. It was certainly the most breathtaking scene I had ever come across. It is Lake Bogoria, in Kenya's Rift Valley.

The first thing that hits you is the scale. The lake, though shallow, is over 18 miles in length. Its backdrop is a dramatic 600-metre-high escarpment. Semi-arid plains extend off to the horizon on either side. Then you see the colours. In the months around the rainy season the land is speckled with green bushes and trees. The lake itself is deep blue. The tinge of pink around the edges turns out on a closer look to be flamingos. This is a favourite spot for them, and flocks of up to 2 million carpet the shores of the lake. It is one of those views you know your camera will never cope with. You can't really take the scenery home, and so you just stand there staring at it, wondering why no-one had ever told you about this before and trying to work out what to do with it now that you've found it. You don't want to take your eyes off it, and you know the moment you walk away there's no chance of remembering it properly.

But Lake Bogoria hides a dark secret. Actually it's not much of a secret – there are signs up all over the place warning you about it. The fact is that, despite all its prettiness, it is a deadly place. For a start it is very, very hot. You are conscious of every single square centimetre of skin that is exposed to the sun. It feels as though you are touching hot metal and you just know that very soon whole swathes of your body will match the colour of the flamingos.

Then there are the animals. There are cheetahs in the area. Forget images of majestic cats perched thoughtfully on high branches; just think of claws and teeth that can bear down on you at 75 miles per hour.

And the water might well look inviting, but this is no place for a quick splash and paddle. The lake is alkaline and hyper-saline. It would be a little like wading into really salty bleach, not somewhere for a refreshing dip, unless you enjoy bathing in industrial-strength window cleaner.

So perhaps we'll stay on dry ground. Except that underneath all this calm beauty is massive geothermal activity. Boiling water bubbles through the earth's surface and geysers shoot sulphur water into the air. The signs telling you to keep out are there for a reason: one misstep and the ground could crumble underfoot, exposing you to the unpleasant turmoil bubbling away just under the surface.

Beauty and hostility – two characteristics that often seem to go together in the natural world. It is something of a paradox, and needless to say our relationship to the environment has perplexed and intrigued us for generations. Some, seeing nature primarily in terms of a utility to be exploited, have had little regard for any environmental damage caused by human development. It is just a matter of resources to be used. Others, seeing the beauty of nature, and the extent to which we depend on it, have tended toward forms of nature-worship. It is a volatile power over us which requires our allegiance. In this case, it might be the human cost of environmental conservation for which they have little regard.

Certainly our relationship to the physical world is complex, and sometimes seems a little like a dysfunctional couple who are unable to live without each other, and yet when together seem only able to hurt each other. This is not the place to delve into current debates about environmentalism. But the resurrection of Jesus Christ and his people has a bearing on all this. And it shouts one particular truth very loudly:

The physical matters to God.

Our bodily future is physical, and so too is our environmental future. God has a plan for the bodies he gave us, and he has a plan for this world. The key to it all is resurrection. But to see where we're going we need to understand where we are. And the key word here is frustration.

Frustration

Paul wants to point us to how creation is bound up with God's plans for us. This shouldn't surprise us: creation has also been bound up with our sin. It is groaning.

> The creation waits in eager expectation for the sons of God to be revealed. For the creation was subjected to frustration, not by its own choice, but by the will of the one who subjected it, in hope that the creation itself will be liberated from its bondage to decay and brought into the glorious freedom of the children of God.
>
> We know that the whole creation has been groaning as in the pains of childbirth right up to the present time.
>
> (Romans 8: 19–22)

Conflict often affects surroundings. When the fight is physical there is all manner of collateral damage: physical things are broken, the whole room can get a make-over. When it is emotional – a marriage falling apart, say – then it spills over into the whole family, and children may be damaged in the process. Conflict rarely, if ever, confines its effects solely to those taking part.

Our conflict with God has affected creation. It has been dragged down with our sin. It often has to bear the brunt of our hostility to God. And in his response to sin, God has subjected it to frustration. It is now out of joint. The world is not as it was meant to be, reminding us that we are not the people we are meant to be. It groans. It quakes. We still have access to the blessings for which God provided this world, but it is also hostile: on the large scale, volcanoes, earthquakes, tsunamis and drought blight the lives of countless individuals. We see it too on a smaller scale. On a recent hike in the hills of Maryland, my host had to explain what to do if we came across one of the various kinds of poisonous snakes sometimes encountered in that area. Nature is not cozy.

Paul also describes creation as being in 'bondage to decay' (Romans 8:21). Just as we have found with our physical body, there is a tendency in the physical world towards disintegration. If I do nothing, my car rusts. It's what the scientists call 'entropy'. Nature, left to its own devices, tends towards decay. It takes huge efforts to arrest this process – like having to wash the car each week – and no effort to let it happen. Matter everywhere seems to be on a downward slide.

In this passage, nature is somewhat personified. It did not choose to be this way, Paul says. It was made subject to frustration by God. The phrase 'as nature intended' may be used to explain any number of things, but it cannot describe the often harsh character of the physical world in which we live. Creation is in frustration. And it longs for more.

Promise

Frustration is not the sum total of nature's experience. Paul describes it at the beginning of this passage as waiting 'in eager expectation' (verse 19). Creation is on tiptoes of excitement, for frustration is not its final destination. It has been subjected 'in hope' (verse 20). There is better to come. Creation has something to look ahead to. We will be finally made right, and so too will all nature. It will be liberated from its frustration, and this liberation is bound up with our final transformation. Nature longs for the 'sons of God to be revealed' (verse 19).

Creation looks ahead to the time when it will be liberated and perfected. As with our resurrection bodies, this new nature will have both continuity and discontinuity with what has gone before.

Discontinuity

The discontinuity is obvious. There will be much that is new. The character of the physical world will have changed. The Bible speaks of 'a new heaven and a new earth' (Revelation 21:1). The one on the throne says, 'I am making everything new!' (Revelation 21:5). This is exactly what had been promised. God had said through Isaiah, 'Behold! I will create new heavens and a new earth. The former things will not be remembered, nor will they come to mind' (Isaiah 65:17). The effect will be that of a superior movie remake: no-one thinks about the original any more – it is surpassed in every respect. The Bible promises radical transformation.

This reminds us that heaven will be physical. Various things surprised me when I first began to look at the Bible's teaching about heaven. For one thing, it will be communal (that is, I won't be 'away from it all' in some nice spot on my own miles from everyone else). Heaven will be perfect human society. It will also be productive (I won't just be having an eternal lie-in).

But the biggest surprise was learning that heaven will be physical. But then virtually none of my mental imagery of heaven had come from the Bible, but from medieval artists and modern-day cartoonists: clouds, harps and winged babies floating around in nightdresses. In fact, part of the blame lies in calling it 'heaven' to start with. It is the new earth. It will be no less physical than the present earth. Our destiny is solid!

And it will be transformed. No death or pain. It's hard for us to imagine, for we have no frame of reference for this.

WHY TV WILL HAVE TO CHANGE

I enjoy natural history, and love watching nature documentaries. Yet for every moment of nobility, every cute creature, every stunning insight into the beauty and ingenuity of the animal world, there is phenomenal gore. For every fluffy, happy example of cuteness, there are corresponding moments of horror as it gets its face bitten off/brain overrun by fungus/sharp claws thrust into it. I can think of one nature programme that has grossed me out more than the bloodiest movies I've ever seen.

How different the new earth will be:

> The wolf will live with the lamb,
>   the leopard will lie down with the goat,
> the calf and the lion and the yearling together;
>   and a little child will lead them.
> The cow will feed with the bear,
>   their young will lie down together,
>   and the lion will eat straw like the ox.
> The infant will play near the hole of the cobra,
>   and the young child put his hand into the viper's nest.
> They will neither harm nor destroy
>   on all my holy mountain,
> for the earth will be full of the knowledge of the LORD
>   as the waters cover the sea.
>   (Isaiah 11:6–9)

It is a picture of beautiful harmony where once there had been hostility.

Continuity

And yet, as I once heard it paraphrased, God says, 'I will make all things new', not 'I will make all new things'. In trying to appreciate the radical change, we must not forget that there will also be significant continuity. The new earth will not be completely unrecognizable. It will still be *this* world – a renewed version of it, not a replacement for it.

A key text for this comes at the end of the narrative of the flood in Genesis chapter 9. God has rescued Noah and his companions, and he now commits himself to creation with the following words: 'I establish my covenant with you: Never again will all life be cut off by the waters of a flood; never again will there be a flood to destroy the earth' (Genesis 9:11).

I used to struggle with this text, for on the surface it seems to offer little comfort. God promises not to destroy the earth again with a *flood*. It's as if he's playing the computer game SimCity and is considering all the remaining options on the Disasters menu. Not a *flood*, but that still leaves earthquakes, fire and a rampaging Godzilla. It almost sounds like it could be a veiled threat.

But the flood was not just an arbitrary form of judgment. It was an act of un-creation. The waters God had separated to form the land were rejoined, and creation returned to its watery chaos. God was undoing his creation, pressing 'Rewind' and reversing it. It was a brand new start, wiping the whole thing clean.

This promise, then, is not merely to refrain from punishing in this way (while leaving other options open). It is a promise to find a way to remove sin without destroying creation. God's salvation for humanity will never be at the expense (if I can put it that way) of creation. God guarantees the future of this physical world. Creation will not be replaced, but renewed. For all its dramatic differences, the new earth will be *this* earth. Jesus looked ahead to 'the renewal of all things' (Matthew 19:28). All that is wrong will be removed and creation will be perfected. What God has made will not be done away with.

BIRTHDAYS, WEDDINGS AND MARATHONS . . .

Creation therefore looks forward to this renewal. As a child, like most other children, I was always unable to sleep the night before Christmas or my birthday. The excitement was just too much. One of my earliest memories is of my dad letting me open one present at about 2am just to ease the tension a little, and of the two of us playing with the toy right there on the floor. Eager expectation.

As a church minister I have the best seat in the house at weddings. The highlight for me is always the entrance of the bride, not just because you get the best view as she makes her way to the front, but because you see the look on the groom's face as she advances towards him. It is one of my favourite moments in life. Eager expectation.

Creation has hope because Christians have hope. Our future is its future. It is a wonderful motivation to keep going in the Christian life.

A friend of mine recently ran the London Marathon. He is at the peak of fitness and very experienced at such things. But there was one point where he really struggled. One part of the route involved crossing the Thames through a pedestrian tunnel. It was not long, just a few hundred metres. And yet it was the part of the route where struggling runners were most likely to give up: there were no onlookers to cheer them on. Along the entire rest of the route there are crowds of spectators who won't let you stop. Removed from that, even for a matter of metres, it becomes a real battle to keep going.

Creation is rooting for us. It is looking forward to our resurrection for its own liberation, and is cheering us on our way: keep going, keep going, keep going!

Persevering

Resurrection means hope. Hope for us and hope for creation. Hope means we can keep going. If we tire we must look to the resurrection. Paul ends his long discussion on the resurrection in 1 Corinthians 15 with these great words:

Therefore, my dear brothers, stand firm. Let nothing move you. Always give yourselves fully to the work of the Lord, because you know that your labour in the Lord is not in vain. (1 Corinthians 15:58)

It is worth keeping going: our hope is certain. There is a new body and a new earth to look forward to. We know it is coming, for Christ has risen from the dead.

There it is – we must memorize this verse. We must let nothing move us. It might be the reactions of other people to our faith that make us want to shift. The raised eyebrow, the sneer, the patronizing comment, the exclusion, or even the physical abuse. Let nothing move you. Don't budge an inch. It is worth keeping going: our hope is certain. There is a new body and a new earth to look forward to. We know it is coming, for Christ has risen from the dead.

OUR 'LABOUR IN THE LORD'

We must give ourselves fully to the 'work of the Lord': our 'labour in the Lord' is not in vain. What is this labour in the Lord? Some take it to mean Christian ministry: Paul is thinking of preaching, leading Bible studies, evangelism and such like. So, the thinking goes, those are the only activities with any eternal value. They secure and build up souls. I don't deny the awesome privilege God gives us in being his colleagues in the great enterprise of making disciples. I don't disagree for a moment that these activities have eternal value. (We'll be looking in the next section about how the resurrection underlines the importance of this task.) But the Bible does not say they are the *only* activities with eternal significance.

The work God entrusted to humanity back in Eden has not been superseded. In fact, the resurrection gives us renewed motivation to do the creation work of developing human societies and stewarding this world: it shows us that *this* world has a future. The good work we do now in this world will not be lost. It is worth doing.

Our labour in the Lord is all the activity God enables us to do for his glory. It might be raising kids, cooking meals, writing a dissertation, preparing a sermon, fixing a bike, tending a patient, composing a symphony or any number of things. To do all that we do for God's glory is going to be worth it, because God's plans – for people as well as creation – will not be thwarted. Such labour is not in vain. We can keep going.

Some of you may lead unglamorous lives. The daily school run, the weekly essay, the morning commute, the repetitive job, the ongoing housework. You look at other Christians doing things that seem much more significant. Maybe they are engaged in some kind of full-time ministry. Maybe their secular job pulls in a mighty salary and they are sought after to lend financial support to various Christian causes. And there you are, stuck in what feels like a monotonous job and with only very modest financial means. Is it really worth it?

The resurrection says, 'Yes!' Any work that benefits human society is an act of worship and glorifies God. It is the work for which we were created, however mundane it has become in some areas. But it is also work that has a future. It is not wasted. If it is being done for the honour of God, it is worth it. The physical resurrection underlines the importance of our physical labour. This world has a future. Our investment in it is not in vain.

We began this chapter with 1 Peter 1:3: 'Praise be to the God and Father of our Lord Jesus Christ! In his great mercy he has given us new birth into a living hope through the resurrection of Jesus Christ from the dead.'

In the resurrection of Jesus this hope has begun to be realized. Its scope includes not just our bodies, but the whole of this world. Jesus anticipated this in his miracles, both in healing the sick and in putting nature around him right. The one who raised the dead also calmed the storm. These are miracles that point ahead, a foretaste of what the new creation and redeemed humanity will be like. In his teaching, so with the events of his life: we look back to Jesus to look forward to our destiny. In his resurrection we are reborn into a new hope, and it lives and breathes with this unshakable certainty: God began the resurrection project, and he will surely finish it.

4

Mission

'I MEAN, we're all the *same*, aren't we?!'

It was said as though it was self-evident, and everyone else who was listening in nodded and made noises of approval. It was the punchline to the discussion, and the matter was settled – at least it was to them. I had that feeling you get when you profoundly disagree, don't know where to start, and now have an audience to contend with.

Adding to the unease was the fact that it was an old family friend whom I'd not seen for a couple of years. Since we'd last met we'd both changed jobs and locations and so we had a lot to catch up on. She was a nominal churchgoer and involved in community projects, and had spent time liaising with both Christian and Muslim groups from the area. I'd asked how that had been working out, given the diversity of the folks involved. And that's when the punchline came in.

I stumbled through a garbled response. I was conscious of the others who were listening in, of how she was thirty years older than me and I didn't want to sound disrespectful, and of how important it was to explain all this as clearly as I could.

My response was flustered, one of those moments you'd love to go back and redo.

But the fact is that comments like hers come up again and again. Australian writer John Dickson described this view once as the 'Chardonnay Myth' of religion today: that different beliefs are all versions of the same thing. They all lead to the same 'god' and all tap into the same spiritual reality, albeit from slightly different angles. Just pick your favourite metaphor: they are different paths up the same mountain, or different blind men poking at the same elephant, each man thinking the creature in front of him is different from the one the others are describing.

Are religions like Chinese people?

It has always struck me as a lazy way to think. It implies a certain distance being kept from each of the religions being discussed – an ignorance, even. It is hard to study the beliefs of Islam and Christianity, say, without realizing that they involve radically different ways of looking at reality. What similarities they share are really only on the surface. At heart they are totally distinct. Saying all religions are the same is just like saying all Chinese people look the same: it just shows that you've never properly got to know any. Spend a decent amount of time with a group of people from any racial background and you won't think they look the same for very long. The insistence that 'they're all the same' may sound tolerant, but in many cases it is little more than laziness.

It can also be an arrogant way to think. Tell people who practise different forms of religion that they are all 'just the same', and the vast majority of them will beg to differ. There may well be striking similarities: they are all engaged in some form of 'spirituality'; they may share certain moral viewpoints or practise some form of meditation or prayer. But that does not make them the same. Claiming this is really saying you know more about the religions of the world than the millions who have given themselves to understanding and practising them.

Laziness and arrogance, perhaps – but what we really need to talk about is the resurrection of Jesus.

When God comes downstairs . . .

One of the reasons why many today believe that all religions have their own toehold on spiritual truth is that such truth is assumed to be abstract and unverifiable. It is all to do with 'upstairs'. We can't know it with certainty. It is not measurable or open to empirical study and scrutiny. We are in no position to arbitrate between different religious claims. It is all 'out there' and beyond our reach. There is no frame of reference. Whatever ultimate reality is, it is beyond our ability to under-stand. Who is really to say which belief system has got it right? Who is to say that in their own way they haven't all got it right? And so, according to this logic, all religions are true.

The resurrection upsets this apple-cart. It deals with this world and with history. Spiritual truth has come 'downstairs'. The resurrection concerns time and space and things that can be scrutinized. A man known as Jesus of Nazareth walked on this earth. Today, Jews believe he was not their Messiah: he lived and died, but did not rise again. Muslims believe Jesus to be one of the great prophets, but no more than a prophet, and certainly not the greatest. They believe he lived, but that, as an esteemed man of God, Jesus could not have been crucified. It just *seemed* to some that he was. Christians believe – and the Bible claims – that Jesus lived, died and rose again from the dead. These three claims – Jewish, Muslim

and Christian – are more than different. They are contradic-
tory. They cannot all be correct. A man cannot have died and
not died. He cannot have been raised from the dead and still
be dead. This is about history and reality as we know it. It is
about someone's physical body, and whether it lies decom-
posed in the soil of Palestine or is exalted in heaven today.

The resurrection intrudes into the world of 'downstairs' –
here, where we live – and makes claims. It pulls the claims
of these three religions on this point down into the world
of the verifiable.

So, teachers are real people . . .

I can still remember the shock when, as a small child, I one
day discovered one of my schoolteachers shopping in the same
supermarket as my family. It had never occurred to me that
schoolteachers were real human beings who needed to do
normal things like shop and eat. I must have assumed they
lived in school all day. (Actually, if memory serves, one or two
looked as though they did.) And yet it turned out that they
existed in our world, and didn't just live in school. It seemed
very strange that I could bump into one of them in my world.

Christianity is concerned with history. It claims that God not
only controls history, but that in the person of Jesus he has
stepped into history and acted within it. Christian claims about
Jesus are not beyond scrutiny. Christian faith is based on what
God has done 'downstairs'. His actions don't belong in the world
of ethereal, nobody-can-really-know abstractions. Someone
is right and someone is wrong. The resurrection overturns
relativism. All religions are not the same, and their beliefs about
the death and resurrection of Jesus are not all true.

But the resurrection shows us more than this. It doesn't just
show the problems that exist with popular notions of religious

'truth': it demonstrates – in our world – what God thinks. God has acted in human history. Deity entered the world, lived and spoke as a man, and died and rose again. He didn't keep himself at arm's length. The resurrection shows us where God has positioned Jesus Christ. And *that* has implications for us all.

Listen to how Paul describes it during a speech he made in Athens: 'For [God] has set a day when he will judge the world with justice by the man he has appointed. He has given proof of this to all men by raising him from the dead' (Acts 17:31).

Jesus is going to judge the whole of humanity. God has proven this. There is no room for doubt or uncertainty. The proof? God has raised Jesus from the dead. His resurrection confronts us with three stark truths: the exaltation of Jesus, the reality of judgment and therefore of the urgency of mission.

The exaltation of Jesus

Jesus has been raised from death to life. He has also been raised from earth to heaven. The resurrection and ascension both reflect how Jesus has been uniquely exalted by God. Paul tells us more:

Your attitude should be the same as that of Christ Jesus:

Who, being in very nature God,
    did not consider equality with God something to be
        grasped,
but made himself nothing,
    taking the very nature of a servant,
    being made in human likeness.
And being found in appearance as a man,
    he humbled himself
    and became obedient to death – even death on a cross!

> Therefore God exalted him to the highest place
>> and gave him the name that is above every name,
> that at the name of Jesus every knee should bow,
>> in heaven and on earth and under the earth,
> and every tongue confess that Jesus Christ is Lord,
>> to the glory of God the Father.
> (Philippians 2:5–11)

Jesus has been exalted. Paul tells us the 'how' and the 'why'.

The 'how' of Jesus' exaltation

How Jesus has been exalted we see from his title: Jesus Christ is *Lord*. If we've been around Christian things for even a short time, we're probably used to Jesus being called 'Lord'. Most likely, the phrase has therefore lost much of its impact. It sounds more like endearment than veneration, let alone worship. I think of the countless times I've sung about the 'little Lord Jesus' laying down 'his sweet head' in the carol 'Away in a Manger'. It is all a little sugary and saccharine.

The word 'lord' in Paul's time was a bit like the word 'sir' in our time. Give it a capital letter and its meaning shifts somewhat. In lower case, our 'sir' is somewhat innocuous. It's what some school kids call their teachers, some retail assistants call their customers, and some business executives call their more important clients. It is a polite form of address. But capitalized, it becomes much more significant. A 'Sir' is more than someone who stands in front of a classroom or walks into a shop or has an impressive portfolio to his name. A 'Sir' is someone who has a title, someone the Queen has exalted.

So too with 'lord'. In New Testament times the word served as either a polite form of address or a title of exaltation. It's what you would have called your father-in-law if you were being polite. But as a title it was much, much more than even our 'Sir' today. As we saw in a previous section, 'the LORD' was the name God gave to his people by which they could address him. Applied to Jesus, 'Lord' was therefore something of a loaded term. Paul says that Jesus has been declared by his resurrection to be the *Lord*. He is not just saying Jesus is now worthy of being regarded with a certain amount of respect. He is calling Jesus God, applying to him all the significance this name carried in the Old Testament. The lordship of Jesus means far more than a qualification and special certificate. It means that Jesus is to be *worshipped*.

Paul's language in this passage from Philippians reflects this. Language used to describe the veneration deserved by God in the Old Testament is applied here to Jesus. He is to be worshipped just as God had been. Consider these words of God given to the prophet Isaiah:

> Turn to me and be saved,
>> all you ends of the earth;
>> for I am God, and there is no other.
> By myself I have sworn,
>> my mouth has uttered in all integrity
>> a word that will not be revoked:
> *Before me every knee will bow;*
>> *by me every tongue will swear.*
> (Isaiah 45:22–23, my emphasis)

Sound familiar? Jesus is given the status and veneration of God himself. God has exalted him. Jesus has the highest name.

What does this mean?

It means that no other name comes remotely close to that of Jesus. Names that are venerated today – Marx, Buddha, Darwin, the Dalai Lama – are *nothing* next to the name of Jesus Christ. It is like trying to impress people with a ditch you've just dug in the dirt with your foot while standing right next to the Grand Canyon. Great as many individuals have been in human terms, Jesus is in a different league. No-one else has been exalted by God in this way. He can be put alongside no-one. *God* has lifted him up, and *God's* reach is higher than anyone else's.

The 'why' of Jesus' exaltation

Back to Philippians: Paul also tells us *why* God has exalted Jesus. As we marvel at what is happening we mustn't miss God's purpose – it is right there in the last clause. *All* this is done 'to the glory of God the Father' (Philippians 2:11).

Put simply, as Jesus is honoured in this way, God is glorified. The worship of Jesus Christ does not take away from the Father in any way – quite the opposite. Jesus is just as much God as God is. God has exalted Jesus so that we might do the same. To worship Jesus *is* to worship God. We cannot do one without the other.

The implications for us and our society are enormous. To glorify God we must exalt and honour Jesus. We must not think we can somehow do God justice while having a lower view of Jesus than he does. Some might say they worship God but have no interest in Jesus, as if he can be cut out of the equation. Others might say that, while they do not worship Jesus, they nevertheless have deep respect for him. I heard recently of one family who have a tradition of raising a glass to Jesus on Christmas Day. They mean it out of genuine respect. But it is not enough – not nearly enough.

Writer and preacher John Stott on one occasion spoke about a debate he'd had with a group of Anglican ministers. They had recently published a book called *The Myth of God Incarnate*, arguing against the traditional Christian understanding of

Jesus as divine. At one point in the discussion Stott asked them outright: 'Do you worship Jesus Christ?'

They replied that, while they followed the ethical teaching of Jesus and revered him greatly as a spiritual leader, they did not worship him.

Stott was unequivocal in his response: *'Then you are not Christians.'*[1]

There is much in this world that we can get away with not being sure on. But on this we need to be crystal clear: you cannot honour God if you do not worship Jesus. He is the one God exults in. To ignore him is to snub God. You cannot have God while being indifferent to God's greatest delight. Irrespective of how nice, well regarded, humble and spiritual you might otherwise consider yourself to be, this is the deal-breaker. If you deny Jesus worship, you deny God: 'No-one who denies the Son has the Father; whoever acknowledges the Son has the Father also' (1 John 2:23).

We cannot please God if we do not worship Jesus. He has been lifted up: God has exalted him. Resurrection is tied to exaltation. Paul has already shown us this: '[Jesus], who as to his human nature was a descendant of David . . . through the Spirit of holiness was declared with power to be the Son of God, by his resurrection from the dead: *Jesus Christ our Lord*' (Romans 1:3–4, my emphasis).

The resurrection demonstrates the exaltation of Jesus.

The reality of judgment

Jesus the Judge

One of the positions to which Jesus has been exalted is that of Judge. He is the one appointed by God to judge humanity on the day of God's choosing. We need to come back to Paul's words from Athens and read them again: 'For [God] has set a day when he will judge the world with justice by the man he has appointed. He has given proof of this to all men by raising him from the dead' (Acts 17:31). It is a massive claim, and hugely unpopular.

For many today, any notion of divine judgment is repellent. To claim that God will one day judge us all is bad enough. To add that Jesus Christ is the one to whom we must all give an account is even worse. Yet Paul claims it to be so. The basis is not his own thinking or intuition, but what God has done in history. All will be judged by Jesus. And God has given proof of this to everyone: Jesus has been raised from the dead.

At first it can be hard to follow Paul's logic. How does the resurrection prove the certainty of judgment? Or that Jesus will act as the Judge? If we think of the resurrection as proof of anything, it is probably something far more general – the proof of God's work in the world, or of how death is not the end. Clearly Paul is making connections that are unfamiliar to us, and so we need to understand how he gets there in his thinking – how and why the resurrection has this meaning for him. Paul is specific. To understand how the resurrection proves God's judgment, we will need to go back a little and understand the nature of that judgment. Then we will be able to see how the resurrection fits into all this.

The goodness of God's judgment

A PARTY WITH A DIFFERENCE

You are invited to a party. It's a celebration, but one with a difference. It's not people doing the celebrating – it's nature. Creation is rejoicing: singing and dancing. We are left to peek through the windows to see what's going on:

> Let the sea resound, and everything in it,
>> the world, and all who live in it.
> Let the rivers clap their hands,
>> let the mountains sing together for joy.
> (Psalm 98:7–8)

It is an amazing picture. The whole of creation is in joyful convulsion: seas, rivers and mountains, everything in the world. What has got creation so excited? If the first surprise was discovering who is doing the celebrating, the second is discovering what it is they're celebrating. The psalm continues:

> Let them sing before the LORD,
>> *for he comes to judge the earth.*
> He will judge the world in righteousness
>> and the peoples with equity.
> (Psalm 98:9, my emphasis)

Yes, you read that right. Creation is celebrating because God is going to judge the earth. And if the imagery is extraordinary, then the motivation behind it is even more so.

WHY JUDGMENT IS GOOD

We generally don't like the idea of judgment. Our experience of human judgment has probably put us off the idea. Judging others is often an appalling thing. The adjective 'judgmental' is only ever used as a pejorative. And so the last thing we would want from God is judgment. 'I like to think of God as loving, not as someone who judges us,' someone says, and everyone else in the room nods in agreement. The trouble is of course that reality doesn't tend to be based on our likes and dislikes.

I live in a town called Maidenhead. I like to think of Maidenhead as a place of unparalleled architectural beauty, where the works of Wren and Roche grace the town centre. If you've ever been to Maidenhead what I've just said will have made you raise an eyebrow or two. Maidenhead isn't quite like that. In fact, it's not at all like that. The statement is true, though: I *do* like to think of Maidenhead that way. As a statement it tells you something about me. But it tells you nothing at all about the reality of where I live.

Whenever people begin a statement about God with, 'I like to think of God as . . . ', they are telling you a certain amount about themselves and nothing at all about God. Reality is not based on our likes and dislikes. We may abhor the idea of a God who judges the earth. All our friends might abhor it too. But it is quite beside the point to end the discussion there, as if God is bound to conform to the expectations some of us have of him. The question is not about what *we* like, but about what *God* has shown us. He has shown us that he is a God who judges. And the noise of the party going on in Psalm 98 seems to suggest we've missed something if we can't imagine how judgment could ever be a good thing.

God judging what he has made is a good thing because it shows he cares about what he has made. He is not indifferent to this world. It matters greatly to him.

LOVE AND INDIFFERENCE

We need to see that the opposite of love is not anger, but indifference. If you are angry with something it is because it matters to you; indifference shows you could not care less.

Imagine it is Monday lunchtime and you're at the canteen where you work or study. You have loaded up your tray and are looking for a place to sit. Someone intercepts you. You vaguely recognize him; he's from another department or faculty. He looks you in the eye and says, 'I need to tell you something: I don't ever want to know you. You know, just in case you were ever thinking of inviting me round or out for an evening. I don't ever want to spend time with you or have anything to do with you. I just thought you should know that.'

How would you react? Pretty bewildered and maybe a little shaken. But life will go on again quite quickly. This person is a virtual stranger, after all. You'll talk about it to your friends and it'll eventually become something you laugh about.

Imagine it's a different Monday; you're at the canteen on your way to a seat and another person intercepts you. This time it is someone you know well. It's your girlfriend. You've been dating for over a year now. You've been on family holidays together and things are going really well. She looks you in the eye and says, 'I need to tell you something: I don't ever want to know you. I don't want to spend time with you or have anything to do with you. I just thought you should know that.'

How would you feel this time?

Profoundly hurt. Confused. Maybe angry. But you wouldn't be indifferent. This is someone who matters to you, someone you love very dearly. And *that* makes all the difference.

The judgment of God is not a contradiction of his love, but an expression of it. Because we matter to him, he will demand an account of our lives and respond accordingly. This is a good thing. It shows that he cares about us and what happens in his world.

When I was at university I remember writing an essay on a subject I particularly cared about. Given its importance for me, I probably took more care over that essay than any other in my course. I read as widely as I could and found writing it painstaking, trying to put my case as well as I could. By the time I handed it in, I was genuinely pleased with it and sent it off with a sense of anticipation I didn't normally have when I submitted papers.

It was never graded. This particular tutor had a busy writing and lecturing workload and it wasn't unheard of for pieces of work to get forgotten or lost under a pile of papers. But I was left feeling somewhat disappointed. My growth and education as a student were evidently not that important. Not to bother grading my work was another way of saying that as a student I didn't really matter. My work had no value or purpose.

For God not to judge us, and for our lives not to be held accountable, would mean that we didn't ultimately matter to him. So the fact that he will one day judge the world is actually a good thing. It means we have value and purpose. It means wrongdoing will not go unpunished. And since God knows all things, fairness and equity are guaranteed. There will be no injustice when this God makes his judgment.

The timing of God's judgment

Crime can often seem to pay. Much injustice in this world seems to go unchecked. Experience seems to contradict the Bible's insistence that God is concerned with righteousness. Where is this justice and fairness? If he is a God who judges, then why doesn't he get on with it?

It comes as a promise. There are sometimes expressions of God's judgment in this life, but his ultimate judgment is not going to come during the course of human history, but at the end of it. A key passage comes at the end of Daniel: 'Multitudes who sleep in the dust of the earth will awake: some to everlasting life, others to shame and everlasting contempt' (Daniel 12:2).

There will be a moment when God raises everyone from the dead to face judgment. This will be a general resurrection of all human beings. Some will then be sent to everlasting life, others to everlasting contempt. It is a stark promise, but it has huge ramifications. It means that death is no escape from judgment.

A number of years ago the former Yugoslav president Slobodan Milosevic died in custody in The Hague before sentencing could be carried out. Relatives of his many victims were devastated. He was accused of genocide, crimes against humanity and war crimes. Yet he seemed to have escaped justice. It was as if he was laughing from beyond the grave, his atrocities unpunished. But the Bible tells a different story: we cannot escape the judgment of God. It will come to us all after death. The expectation we are left with from Daniel's words above is that there will be a resurrection of all people at which they will receive the just judgment of God. Death is no escape from this – quite the opposite.

This helps us understand the perspective of Jesus' friend Martha in John 11. Her brother Lazarus has died. She knows that Jesus has the power of God, and Jesus assures her that Lazarus will rise again. She responds, 'I know he will rise again in the resurrection at the last day' (John 11:24).

She got the wrong end of the stick. Jesus was promising that Lazarus was going to be raised by him at that very moment. But it shows us the mental furniture of someone like Martha at that time. She believed there was going to be a resurrection at the last day that would involve everyone, hence her brother would rise again then. That was her expectation from the Old Testament.

The resurrection of Jesus was therefore an anomaly, not because people had no concept of resurrection (far from it, as Martha illustrates) but because Jesus was raised, alone, in the middle of history and not with everyone else at the end of it. He was raised before the rest of us. And the explanation is clear from what Jesus says to Martha next: 'I am the resurrection and the life. He who believes in me will live, even though he dies' (John 11:25).

Jesus has a different relationship to the final, general resurrection than everybody else. He *is* the resurrection. It is his domain, his patch. He is its instigator. In his rising, the starting pistol has been fired and the resurrection age has begun.

We find this message on the lips of the apostles in the early days of the Christian church. In fact, it was so central to their message that it was what they became known for.

> The priests and the captain of the temple guard and the Sadducees came up to Peter and John while they were speaking to the people. They were greatly disturbed because the apostles were teaching the people and *proclaiming in Jesus the resurrection of the dead*.
>
> (Acts 4:1–2, my emphasis)

That was their message. In Jesus we see the resurrection of the dead. It has started to happen.

The certainty of God's judgment

We can begin to see the logic behind Paul's statement in Athens. Judgment will come at the end with the resurrection of the dead. Resurrection and judgment are linked. The resurrection of Jesus anticipates the resurrection to come and indicates that his place in the matter is unique. He *is* the resurrection. His is the judgment. He is the man God has appointed.

This judgment is going to be universal. Look again at the words of Paul, this time starting a little earlier:

> In the past God overlooked such ignorance, but now he commands all people everywhere to repent. For he has set a

day when he will judge the world with justice by the man he has appointed. He has given proof of this to all men by raising him from the dead.

(Acts 17:30–31)

Notice Paul's use of 'all'. All are to repent. The whole world will face the judgment of Jesus. God has given proof of this to all men. The scope is universal. It concerns everyone who has ever lived. All need to repent because all have turned away from God. All will be judged because God has made us all. We are his work of creation. His is the right to call us to account for our lives. The nature of that judgment to come is implied in the warning to repent. Everyone has naturally lived in the wrong direction.

This was the first public message we heard from Jesus. At the start of his ministry, as he 'went live', this was his message: 'The time has come,' he said. 'The kingdom of God is near. Repent and believe the good news!' (Mark 1:15).

WHEN GOD CALLS 'TIME!'

The kingdom of God has arrived in the coming of Jesus, and by his resurrection the judgment of God is anticipated and begun. When the barman rings the bell and calls 'Time!' it means that closing up has started. Any remaining business needs to be done *now*. Very soon it will be too late. In the resurrection of Jesus, God has called 'Time!' on the world. The end-time judgment has begun: a man has been raised from the dead. Now is the time to do business with God, to get in the right with him. Soon it will be too late.

We have already seen that one day every knee will bow before Jesus: every Muslim knee, every Hindu knee, every agnostic knee, every atheist knee. Everyone we have worked with and lived beside. Everyone we went to school with and can't remember the name of. Everyone who shares our surname, who watches the same TV show, who cuts us off in traffic, serves us in a restaurant or asks us for money. There is absolutely no doubt this is going to happen. They have the opportunity to bow voluntarily now before a Saviour, or compulsorily then before a Judge. If at this point they are still hostile to Jesus then we know what happens next:

They have the opportunity to bow voluntarily now before a Saviour, or compulsorily then before a Judge.

> The LORD says to my Lord:
>   'Sit at my right hand
> until I make your enemies
>   a footstool for your feet.'
> (Psalm 110:1)

The most tragic moment in all of history will be when Jesus puts his feet up. It is impossible to resist him and win.

Judgment is real. Jesus has been raised from the dead.

The necessity of mission

The best kind of movie ending

There are two kinds of movie ending. One kind feels as though the writers are making it up as they go. So come the climax, they end up pulling something quite improbable out of the hat to finish it all up: a sudden revelation that is out of kilter with all that's happened before, or the main protagonist leaping suddenly to his feet even though he has about twenty-three bullets in his chest. It feels artificial and bolted on, a device to get us to the end credits and then back home in time for dinner.

The second kind of ending is much better. It ties up the threads of the movie in a way that is consistent even if it might be a little unexpected. One thinks of the end to the classic *The Shawshank Redemption*. It makes sense of what has come before rather than undermining it. You're left with the feeling that it couldn't have ended any other way.

At first glance, the end of Matthew's Gospel feels like the first kind. Jesus says:

> Therefore go and make disciples of all nations, baptising them in the name of the Father and of the Son and of the Holy Spirit, and teaching them to obey everything I have commanded you. And surely I am with you always, to the very end of the age.
> (Matthew 28:19–20)

It feels a little bolted on. It's as if Matthew anticipated all those 'Missionary Sundays' that churches would be running in the centuries to come, and so tacked this on at the end to give us something to wheel out after the slide-show of the new church roof going on in Zambia. It seems, at first glance, out of kilter with the events that have formed the climax of the Gospel. After the drama of the trial, execution and resurrection of Jesus we are suddenly dropped into a 'Missionary Sunday' moment.

We need to think again. The final section of Matthew (known as the 'Great Commission' for reasons that are obvious) is actually the climax of the whole Gospel. It couldn't have ended any other way. Far from being a change of gear, it is actually consistent with the direction Matthew has been charting for the previous twenty-seven chapters. We don't even need to go back to chapter 1: the first half of chapter 28 shows us why the second half is there.

The risen Lord's business

The chapter begins with a scene that is at once poignant and ordinary: 'After the Sabbath, at dawn on the first day of the week, Mary Magdalene and the other Mary went to look at the tomb' (Matthew 28:1). The ordinariness of this does not last long. Three overwhelming events happen in quick succession.

MEETING LIGHTNING

The first is the arrival of an angel:

> There was a violent earthquake, for an angel of the Lord came down from heaven and, going to the tomb, rolled back the stone and sat on it. His appearance was like lightning, and his clothes were white as snow. The guards were so afraid of him that they shook and became like dead men.
> (Matthew 28:2–4)

Forget your mental image of angels. Forget a rosy-cheeked, effeminate face. Forget the bed sheet and tinsel costume. This angel looked like lightning: ablaze with the devastating mega-wattage of God's holiness. The guards, hardened soldiers who would not have been the jumpiest human specimens on earth, convulsed and became as dead. This angelic encounter alone would be enough for these two women to dine out on for years to come. But this was just the beginning of it all.

The next shock is what the angel says to the two women:

The angel said to the women, 'Do not be afraid, for I know that you are looking for Jesus, who was crucified. He is not here; he has risen, just as he said. Come and see the place where he lay. Then go quickly and tell his disciples: "He has risen from the dead and is going ahead of you into Galilee. There you will see him." Now I have told you.'
(Matthew 28:5–7)

'He is not here.' 'He has risen.' Two statements that would change everything for ever.

As the women were no doubt reeling from this, the angel showed them where Jesus had lain. What they were struggling to take in aurally, the angel would confirm to them visually. Jesus really was not there. In fact, his disciples would find him in Galilee, and this the two Marys were charged with telling them.

These women were the first to hear of the resurrection. They had monumental news. They were completely overwhelmed. They ran off on their task to reach the disciples, we're told, 'afraid yet filled with joy' (Matthew 28:8). There was so much to take in. It must be hard to run while at the same time staggering. And yet they were about to be floored by a third shock.

Jesus turns up:

Suddenly Jesus met them. 'Greetings,' he said. They came to him, clasped his feet and worshipped him. Then Jesus said to them, 'Do not be afraid. Go and tell my brothers to go to Galilee; there they will see me.'
(Matthew 28:9–10)

Worship, adoration and fear. But Jesus confirms their task. Tell the disciples. Galilee. They'll see me.

DESTINATION GALILEE

Three monumental things have just happened – and it's not even breakfast-time. Yet from these encounters it is clear what is on the agenda of the risen Jesus: Galilee. Everyone is to trudge all the way up to Galilee. That's the place the disciples are to meet him, not here in Jerusalem. It all has to happen in Galilee. Now that he's risen, that's the place to find him.

Places often have symbolic significance. Under the Nazis, the German city of Nuremberg became the focal point of state propaganda and rule, through the rallies held there and the anti-Semitic 'Nuremberg Laws' signed there. When it came to deciding the location of the post-war international tribunals, the Allies chose Nuremberg, in part for its symbolism. This would be a fitting place where justice could be decided for those at the centre of the Nazi regime.

So what is the significance of Galilee? An important prophecy from Isaiah has the answer: 'Nevertheless, there will be no more gloom for those who were in distress. In the past he humbled the land of Zebulun and the land of Naphtali, but in the future he will honour *Galilee of the Gentiles*' (Isaiah 9:1, my emphasis).

Galilee of the Gentiles – literally, Galilee 'of the nations'. The geography of Israel and its surroundings was such that invading forces would sweep down from the north. Galilee would be the first place hit. Though it was a lush and fertile region, it became known as 'the land of the shadow of death' (Isaiah 9:2). Yet in this place of darkness Isaiah had a vision of a new light dawning. There would be a new invasion, one of a very different kind. God was about to flood the land with salvation and life. Rather than being an invasion *from* the nations, it would be *to* them. The increase of this perfect government would not end (see Isaiah 9:7).

Galilee of the nations. This was the risen Lord's business. And it was to be the launch pad of the risen Lord's mandate.

The risen Lord's mandate

Jesus is raised from the dead and makes a beeline for Galilee of the nations. What happens next should therefore come as no surprise.

> Then Jesus came to them and said, 'All authority in heaven and on earth has been given to me. Therefore go and make disciples of all nations, baptising them in the name of the Father and of the Son and of the Holy Spirit, and teaching them to obey everything I have commanded you. And surely I am with you always, to the very end of the age.'
> (Matthew 28:18–20)

This is his mandate: universal disciple-making.

It is bound up with *who he is*. Jesus has been exalted. Through his resurrection and ascension the King has been enthroned. All authority has been given to him. The universe is his. His authority is absolute and exhaustive. You will never breathe air that doesn't belong to him and you will suffocate if you try. You will never visit a place over which he is not rightfully Lord. It is not that his power is restricted to one or two places where he is especially known and followed. It is not that he has only a toehold of control in some areas. The whole world is his by right. And so the whole world needs to be alerted to that fact. He is the Ruler, the King. *All* authority is his. Therefore we go to *all* nations. His reign is global and so our concern is not to be parochial.

World mission is therefore not an optional Christian hobby for some. Jesus' concern is to be our concern, and that involves having a concern for the whole world. The progress of the gospel to and among the nations is to be on the heart of all believers. If Jesus is the risen Lord then this has to matter to us.

It is bound up with *what he requires*. Jesus is seeking disciples, not just converts. He is looking for men and women who will be mature in the faith, rooted and established in him. Not just a list of names of those who came forward at a rally or prayed a prayer of commitment. Not hit-and-run evangelism. Young believers are to be nurtured and strengthened. All Christ's people are to be edified: built up in him. Unreached people are to be reached, and reached people are to be helped to grow.

Notice that this is a task we are all to be involved in. These new disciples are to be taught to obey everything Jesus had commanded his original hearers, and that includes this command to make disciples. This command is to be passed down with the gospel. Each successive generation of Christians is to pick up where the previous generation left off.

It is bound up with *what he promises*. Soon Jesus will be taken up to heaven and his Spirit poured out on his people. By that Spirit he promises to be with us, universally and permanently. By his Spirit he equips us all to serve this commission. We will have different roles and gifts. But all of us can be encouraged that we have a part to play.

ATTITUDE, NOT GEOGRAPHY

Mission is about attitude, not geography; what we're doing, not where we are; a particular priority, not a particular place. It is about an attitude that has come to terms with the resurrection of Jesus and what that means for the world. God has exalted him to be worshipped. He is confirmed as the Judge of all, and in his rising the day of that judgment has been fixed and confirmed. People need to be reached with his gospel of forgiveness, hope and new life.

If we come to terms with this it will affect how we use the resources God has given us. The language you have grown up speaking might be an opening into a country where conventional missionaries have no access. Most who read this speak English as your first language. The world population can be pretty much split into those who can speak English and those who are trying to. There are more people learning English in China than speaking it in the United States.

Or think about education. Some of us will have been privileged enough to receive good degrees that can open doors to many parts of God's world. Or think about money. Most Christians in this world will never have enough money to get on a plane even once in their lifetime. Or think about resources. Christians in the West have access to training and literature that is the best in the world.

Wherever we go and whomever we work with, it must be for the right reasons. The motivation for all this is the exaltation of Jesus. Whether our 'going' is down the street or across the continents, it is because Jesus has been exalted.

LEARNING THE RIGHT KIND OF JEALOUSY

There is a form of jealousy that is right and proper. It is the resentment of a rival who has no place being there – someone who is taking something that is ours by right. Most forms of jealousy we encounter are unwarranted and deeply unattractive, and so the word has almost totally negative associations. It takes effort on our part to recognize the goodness of jealousy when it is called for. If a third party intrudes into a marriage, for example, then it is right and healthy for the spouse to be jealous – he or she has a right to an exclusive relationship with the marriage partner.

God has a right to supreme renown. He is deserving of our exclusive worship. There is a form of jealousy that is therefore godly. It is found in God himself and should also be found in those who follow him.

UNDERSTANDING EZEKIEL IN THAILAND

I was sitting in the lobby of a youth hostel in central Thailand a few years ago. I was part of a team teaching English for the summer. For the first couple of mornings I was waking up far too early due to jet lag, and the lobby seemed to be the only place to sit and read without disturbing everyone else. It so happened that on this particular morning I was reading a couple of chapters of Ezekiel. Unbeknown to me, the manager of the hostel was looking over my shoulder with curiosity. He eventually asked me what I was reading and why. I explained it was part of the Old Testament and that I tried to read something of Scripture every morning to give me something to chew on for the rest of the day.

'I wish I could do something like that!' he suddenly announced. 'Please, tell me something from what you are reading for me to think about today.'

I didn't really know where to start. I was in the middle of Ezekiel and I was a little perplexed. I'd only met this man when checking in the night before. He was a Buddhist from a culture very different from mine, and he'd probably never looked at a Bible before.

I looked again at the chapters I'd just been reading, appalled at how little I'd taken in. I was wondering what on earth to share with this man when I noticed something. There was a phrase being repeated again and again. I hadn't really noticed it on the first read, yet here it was, cropping up all over the place. It seemed to come at the end of virtually every paragraph, and as I flipped over the next few pages I realized these same words were shot through the whole book like letters in a stick of rock: 'Then they will know that I am the

LORD.' (For a chapter and verse reference, flick open Ezekiel to just about any page and you'll soon find it.)

I wasn't entirely sure of the specifics of what God was up to in the passage before me, but it was pretty clear what his purpose was. God's desire was to be known. He wanted them (his people, and also the surrounding nations looking in over the fence) to know who he was. That is the ultimate reason for his acts of salvation and judgment. He is a God of enormous glory. Not to know him is not just regrettable; it is culpable. It is a scandal to heaven when God is not known. What my new Buddhist friend made of this I've no idea, but it hit me like a sledgehammer.

Look carefully at the following:

> Therefore say to the house of Israel, 'This is what the Sovereign LORD says: It is not for your sake, O house of Israel, that I am going to do these things, but for the sake of my holy name, which you have profaned among the nations where you have gone. I will show the holiness of my great name, which has been profaned among the nations, the name you have profaned among them. Then the nations will know that I am the LORD, declares the Sovereign LORD, when I show myself holy through you before their eyes.'
> (Ezekiel 36:22–23)

God's heart is laid bare in this passage. It might come as a surprise to us, but he is not working primarily for the sake of his people. His chief concern is for his name. His top priority is his reputation. God is jealous.

This is the perspective he wants his people to share. Think about what we pray for. My tendency is often to treat prayer like room service: here are all the things that would be quite nice today, please. Though we can pray about anything, there are nevertheless priorities Jesus gives us for our prayer life. We call it the Lord's Prayer.

The words are so familiar that the impact is often lost on us. Jesus tells us what to pray for: what matters most to him. And the very first thing we are to pray for is God's name. We are to pray it would be hallowed. (Not 'Harold', as one little boy I know used to think.) For something to be hallowed, it is to be thought about with awe.

WHY THE WHITE HOUSE CAUSES SLEEPLESSNESS

For a number of years I've been interested in American politics. I think it's a combination of the scale and grandeur that first got me interested, but then I began to learn about the history of it all. A couple of American friends showed me round the House of Representatives in Washington DC and talked me through the origins of the political system. Since then, I've been hooked, avidly following each successive election campaign, reading up on the main characters from each party and learning more and more about the history of the presidency. Among my most prized possessions is a set of prints of George Washington and Thomas Jefferson.

So you'll begin to appreciate that I didn't get much sleep the night before my first visit to the White House. My tour had been booked months in advance. I'd read so much about this place and what it represented. And here I was walking through its corridors. To me, at least, this was *hallowed* turf.

God longs that his name – who he is – will have this kind of effect on people, that they will hold it in the highest regard; consider it special and precious. He asks us to pray it would be so. His reputation is meant to matter to us. He wants Jesus to be known.

PAUL'S GREATEST MOTIVATION

We see this perspective in Paul. At the beginning of his letter to the Romans, Paul is setting out his stall. He explains what he's about: what his gospel is and where it comes from.

> Paul, a servant of Christ Jesus, called to be an apostle and set apart for the gospel of God – the gospel he promised beforehand through his prophets in the Holy Scriptures regarding his Son, who as to his human nature was a descendant of David, and who through the Spirit of holiness was declared with power to be the Son of God by his resurrection from the dead: Jesus Christ our Lord. Through him and for his name's sake, we received grace and apostleship to call people from among all the Gentiles to the obedience that comes from faith.
> (Romans 1:1–5)

Undergirding all of it is the name of Jesus. Paul's special calling as an apostle, all his ministry, hardships, travel, prayers and writings – all of it is for the sake of Jesus' name.

WANTING JESUS TO BE FAMOUS

We see the same perspective in the other apostles. Facing violent persecution from the religious authorities in Jerusalem, they rejoiced. Why? ' . . . because they had been counted worthy of suffering disgrace for the Name. Day after day, in the temple courts and from house to house, they never stopped teaching and proclaiming the good news that Jesus is the Christ' (Acts 5:41–42). They were driven, even in the teeth of ferocious opposition, by a love of the Name. Their concern was for the reputation of Jesus.

This was the perspective of some of the first Christian missionaries, too. John describes them as those who had been sent out 'for the sake of the Name' (3 John 7).

Our uppermost concern in all that we do is to be the reputation of Jesus. We seek to spread the gospel not because people have a right to hear it, but because he has the right to be known. Jesus alone has been raised to the highest place of honour.

We have a mission because of his resurrection.

Further Reading

Assurance

Mark Meynell, *Cross-Examined* (IVP, 2005)
John Stott, *The Cross of Christ* (IVP, 2006)

Transformation

Tim Chester, *You Can Change* (IVP, 2008)
Vaughan Roberts, *Distinctives* (Authentic Media, 2000)

Hope

Adrian Warnock, *Raised with Christ* (Crossway, 2010)

Mission

John Dickson, *Promoting the Gospel* (Aquila, 2006)
John Piper, *Let the Nations be Glad* (IVP, 2003)

Notes

Introduction

1. From a transcript of his debate with John Lennox: The God Delusion Debate, The Alys Stephens Center, Birmingham, Alabama, 3 October 2007. Hosted by the Fixed Point Foundation.

Chapter Two: Transformation

1. <http://www.urbandictionary.com/define.php?page=5 &term=atheism> accessed 20 May 2009.
2. C. S. Lewis, *Prince Caspian* (HarperCollins, 1980), p. 124.
3. Source unknown.

Chapter Four: Mission

1. John Stott, 'Every Knee Shall Bow', sermon preached at All Souls Church, Langham Place, London, 19 August 1984.